The C · A · T PSYCHOLOGIST

MARDIE MacDONALD

Stoddart

To Miss Tits, the Queen of Cats, and to Tiger, Toby,
Samantha, Sabastian, Kitty and Gaerdo, our jewels in the
cat crown, and to their devoted servants, Margaret, Spence,
Dan, Ronald Christopher, Ruth and Kathryn

First published in 1990 by
Stoddart Publishing Co. Limited
34 Lesmill Road
Toronto, Canada
M3B 2T6

CANADIAN CATALOGUING IN PUBLICATION DATA

MacDonald, Mardie
    The cat psychologist

ISBN 0-7737-2273-4

1. Cats - Psychology.   2. Cats - Behavior.
I. Title.

SF446.5.M33 1990   636.8'001'9   C89-090622-X

Text Illustrations: Kathryn Adams
Typesetting: Tony Gordon Ltd.
Printed in Canada on acid-free paper.

The author and publisher would like to thank ORBIS, a division of Macdonald & Co. (Publishers) Ltd., for permission to reprint from *The Cat Care Question and Answer Book* by Dr. Barry Bush, BVSc, Ph.D., FRCVS, copyright © 1981.

CONTENTS

Introduction:
What Is a Cat Psychologist?   *3*

1   The Pet of the Nineties:
The Nature of Your Cat   *17*

2   Cats in Crisis:
Stress and Your Cat   *35*

3   Can You Pass the Cat Test?
Living with Your Cat   *73*

4   Your Cat's Well-Being:
How to Care for Your Cat   *89*

5   New Frontiers:
You Can Make a Difference   *131*

Further Reading   *136*

Index   *137*

ACKNOWLEDGMENTS

Very special thanks to Angel Guerra of Stoddart Publishing for believing in me; Shaun Oakey, my editor, for understanding the cat and understanding me; and all the cats, and their people, whom I have worked with through the years.

. . . .

I do believe that all God's creatures have the right to live as much as we have. Instead of prescribing the killing of the so-called injurious fellow creatures of ours as a duty, if men (or women) of knowledge had devoted their gift to discovering ways of dealing with them otherwise than by killing them, we would be living in a world befitting our status as men (women) — animals endowed with reason and the power of choosing between good and evil, right and wrong, violence and non-violence, truth and untruth.

— Mahatma Gandhi
Mohan-Mala — A Gandhian Rosary

Introduction:

What Is a Cat Psychologist?

THE TORONTO *GLOBE AND MAIL* writes in its business section about "The Cat on Madison Avenue," noting the billions of dollars generated when the cat is used in advertising. From Volvos to toilet tissues, from Coke to business machines, the 5 million cat owners in Canada, the 55 million in the United States and the one in every three European households where a cat lives are bombarded with "kitty commercials."

Mila Mulroney, the wife of Canada's prime minister, entertains the wives of world leaders in Toronto for the 1988 Economic Summit. She takes them to visit a children's hospital, where, before television news cameras from around the world, she reads the children a story. What kind of story does she choose? What else? A cat story — *Can You Catch Josephine?* by Canada's Stéphane Poulin.

Prince Edward visits Canada, and what do we give this royal visitor as a special treat? A private viewing of the musical *Cats*, already a hit worldwide — even in Russia, where reviewers called *Koshki* a "holiday for the soul."

The world over, the cat is now being taken into jails, mental institutions, homes for the elderly and hospitals to work her own brand of "cat magic," with wonderful results. Just being with a cat perks everybody up — fevers go down, depressions lift and anxiety and anger are forgotten.

From business to pleasure, the cat is always there for us, and has been for a long, long time. According to some archaeologists, cats go back 100,000 years and were domesticated by the Egyptians about 5,000 years ago. What a history of change! Whether worshipped as a god or hated as an incarnation of the devil, the cat is never boring. All over the world she takes centerstage.

Yet all over the world, millions of cats are put to sleep every single year because of what are called "behavioral problems." Much as we love cats, we far too often fail to understand them.

Which is where I come in.

A young man asked me the other day, why would anyone want to be a *cat psychologist*? Well, first of all, I love cats. Nothing is more fun and uplifting than being with a cat. She gives us so much more than we give her. Great writers and artists have for hundreds of years portrayed the beauty and joys that abound in the cat. I feel them equally extraordinary.

Cats have given me so much over the years, and today they are in desperate need of help. I would be disloyal if I did not do all I could for them. I hope that by writing this book I can save some of those cats who are in trouble. With so many cats being put down every year, the need is great for a common-sense, up-to-date feline-behavior book with lots of advice and answers.

I tell you about your cat's psychological needs and *your* psychological needs, to help you adapt to each other's ways. I discuss diet, exercise, declawing, spaying and neutering, the needs of indoor and outdoor cats and my plans for "safe houses" for abandoned cats and free cat care for those people who can't afford vets' fees. My book is for the cat owner and the cat-owner-to-be. It deals with preventive cat care and not sickness; it offers refreshing solutions that involve no chemicals or medicines, so that you, in your own home, can learn to guide your cat along the route to emotional health. Whether your cat is in her natural habitat (outside) or an unnatural habitat (inside), I show you how to cope so that you and your cat will always be happy and will constantly have fun together.

In short, as Canada's only "feline behaviorist," I am going

to tell you how to look after your cat so that the quality of her life will be the best possible within the environment you have provided for her. Following my common-sense cat advice and always keeping in mind the cat's nature will prevent your cat from becoming a disposable item in a throw-away society.

There has never been a period in my life when I haven't had a cat or cats around me. When I was growing up, there were always litters of kittens in our home, and my brother, Dan, and I would fight over which kittens we wanted to take to bed for the night. When we woke up they were back with their mother, of course, but what fun and comfort to have those little warm bodies under the covers with us as we drifted off to sleep.

Our family cats were in paradise. We lived in a big house with a very large garden, and they were free to come and go. They played their kitty games in among the flowerbeds and bushes, and we would often find them dozing in the sunshine. As I grew older, it seemed to me no family could be complete without a cat.

After I married and we moved into our first home, deciding when to get a cat for my young son, Ronald, was taken out of my hands one evening when the door flew open and I heard him shout, "Mom, here's a cat. Don't let it out!" And off he went. I looked into the anxious eyes of a twelve-week-old long-haired stray, and it was love at first sight.

Somewhere we got the idea it was a boy, probably from my son, who thought that all cats were boys, so we named it Johnny-go-Round after his favorite storybook character. Later, finding Johnny-go-Round big with kittens turned the name into Misfits, which somehow slipped into Miss Tits. We didn't mean to be rude, but the family cat was stuck with a name that was infamous in the neighborhood. Calling her in at night tended to attract attention.

For fifteen years she was my comfort and best friend. She was loved dearly by all the little boys who came to call on my son every day. She was the watchcat of her territory, and heaven help any animal that came onto her property unasked. She was the ultimate hunter and presented us with a daily offering no matter what we did to stop her. Once she brought in a complete mole's nest, with the baby moles still inside. We rescued many such trophies of hers! She loved us all madly, especially my son, and every night she would go to bed with him. The moment he fell asleep, though, she would jump lightly down and go about her cat business, making sure her house and her garden were in order. Through all those years, she gave our house the soul that a catless house just does not have.

After many years of devoting myself to being a full-time wife and mother, that moment arrived when everyone was gone. I had to start a new life. But doing what? And how? A strong business background and an entrepreneurial spirit, which had never been needed before, were two assets I had. And I had my house. Some very creative thinking was required and that is just what I did.

Some years earlier I had taken in the babies of unwed mothers to give them a good start in life. I began to think, if I could baby-sit children in my home, why not cats? I loved them, too, and knew all there was to know — or so I thought! I began to do my research, phoning all over the city to find out what facilities were available for cat-sitting.

There were none — only cages at the vet's or cages at a kennel. Cat people do not like to put their cats in cages. I know, because I would never do it. I knew I was in business.

I put ads in all the papers, calling my enterprise the Cats' Cradle, a "bed and breakfast" for cats. I would look after my visiting cats just like babies in a cradle. They would be safe and happy in my home. Since the cat's ways and feelings are as natural to me as my own, I knew this would be something I would enjoy and love. In my letter to prospective clients I wrote: "In my own home I give loving, pampered care to your cat while you are on holidays, business trips, moving, etc. During their stay at the Cats' Cradle, your cats receive their favorite food, a screened-in porch for fresh air and bird watching and, best of all, *no cages of any kind*."

The response was fantastic. Little did I know I was about to start my in-depth, hands-on training as North America's only cat psychologist.

For three years, 365 days a year, I lived with hundreds of different cats. Although I had originally planned to take in only seven at a time, the numbers grew. Usually there were about twenty-five guests at any given moment, but I could have filled three or four houses. There were black ones, striped ones, orange ones, fat ones, thin ones, Burmese, Siamese and ones with no tails. They came in limos, compacts, station wagons, taxis. They arrived in cardboard cartons, airline carriers, wire cages, wicker hampers. They also came complete with all their accoutrements — kitty beds, comforters, old socks, scratching posts, catnip mice, kitty candies, furr-ball medicine and cases of expensive cat food. Some owners brought three or four pages of typewritten instructions. Some wanted to see what other males were there in case of fights. Many told me how their cats would act, and they were right on the button. But all those cats had one thing in common: they were brought by loving and devoted owners who were so glad to have found their darlings such a nice home away from home.

What fun it was, and how I wished it did not have to end. However, seven days a week, with no time off, is not good for you even if you do love what you are doing. I also developed painful arthritic spurs on my elbows, which were aggravated by the physical labors of tending to twenty-five litter boxes every day and cleaning, feeding and caring for so many animals. The painful decision had to be made. I sold my home, closed the Cats' Cradle and retired to my getaway spot in Mexico.

At least, I *thought* I was ready to retire!

A few years later, missing my only son and not having enough to occupy my mind, I decided to give the big city another try. Again I faced a major career decision, but I knew that whatever I chose would still have to involve cats. Caring for them physically was out of the question, but I had three years of hands-on experience and had learned more about the cat than I had ever dreamed possible. So why not, I thought, deal with the cat's psyche? Could I help people with their cats' behavior?

In all the time I had been retired, the cat population had been growing like mad. People had problems, and their cats had problems. There was a demand for someone who studied the science of the cat's nature — a cat psychologist. I was in business again.

I put a simple statement in the classified section of *Toronto Life* magazine: "The Cat Psychologist specializes in all feline behavioral problems." The day it appeared, I came home to find on my answering machine calls from one major radio network, one major American TV network, a well-known journalist and several people whose cats had behavioral problems. I was so taken aback by the media attention that I said no, especially to TV — that I knew I did not want. It took me some weeks to realize that if I was going to succeed at this thing I had worked so hard at, I would be foolish indeed to pass up any publicity opportunities, so I said yes to everything. I was soon comfortable in radio and television studios alike.

I was also taken aback by the number of people out there who were in deep trouble with their cats and had no one to turn to. Their questions ranged from diet to scratching posts, kittens to litter, declawing to teeth cleaning. I enjoyed my work so much that I would take all the time my clients wanted, both on the phone and at their homes. My love for cats, my sympathy for their troubles and my desire to continue my life of problem solving, always my forte, helped me through this busy beginning.

Although my "Kitty Calls" to my clients' homes were important, I quickly recognized I could reach so many more people through TV, radio and print. Today my TV appearances are broadcast across Canada and the States. That's a lot of cat owners to reach at once. The same goes for national radio call-in shows. And if callers can't get through to talk about their specific cat problems they often hear me discuss a similar problem with someone else. My newspaper and magazine articles are picked up by wire services and carried all across North America to big-city dailies and small-town weeklies.

In a typical week I do one or two radio interviews and "cat chat" programs, broadcast by various stations across North America and often conducted over the phone right from my own living room. Sometimes I speak at a senior citizens' home or hold an open house at a pet supply store. Every day is different and exciting.

Most of my week is spent going on my Kitty Calls. When the cat owner phones or writes to me with a cat problem, I first determine that it is a behavioral problem, not a physical one. I am not a vet, and I do not dispense veterinary advice. Usually by the time people contact me they have tried everything to solve their problem — with no success — and will have to have their cat put down if I cannot come up with the answers. The Canadian writer Sidney Katz has called me "the lady of last resort" — and that is what I am.

Over the telephone I take down general information on the problem and set up an appointment. I like everyone in the household to sit in on the session if they can, and usually they do. Teenagers, sometimes the cleaning lady or the maid, young children, visiting relatives — anyone who is concerned or who deals with the cat daily. I must have at least one hour of their time, and usually end up staying for two.

I feel the main purpose of my visit is to advise the people how to make the cat as happy as possible within the context of what I find in that particular household and working within the family's lifestyle.

I come prepared with a list of pertinent questions, such as: What does your cat eat? Is she an inside or outside cat? Is she declawed or natural? What changes were there in her life before the problem began? Describe the lifestyle of the household. And so on. When I have all the answers I put the pieces of the puzzle together and come up with the reason the cat is behaving the way she is. Then I take a tour of the house to see what the cat's natural (or unnatural) habitat is.

I usually know quite early in the session what the treatment will be, for although cats' problems vary and they come by their problems differently, the treatment is in most instances the same. Still, it is important that the cat's owners understand how and why their cat developed a particular problem so they can control or avoid the situation in the future. I do not like to leave a session until I am sure they have everything straight in their minds about what should be done. I leave a list of recommendations and let the owners know that I am on call, any time of the day or night, if they have other questions or if other problems develop. One house call is usually sufficient, two at the most.

No matter how people get my verbal cat medicine — whether through TV, radio, print or my Kitty Calls — the main thing is they get the help they need from a cat person with fifty years' experience living with cats, combined with several years' hands-on, in-depth work with them and, by now, three years of cat therapy.

And I can honestly say all my clients' cats have been helped by my natural approach to feline behavioral problems.

All my Kitty Calls are interesting in their own way, though some stand out more than others. I was once hired to find out why a Burmese named Cicero would not come out of the closet. His owner had tried everything to get him out and back with the family. What was wrong? He would not talk to me. He crouched in his closet and looked at me through sad and droopy eyes, hoping I would go away. It turned out his house had been robbed. Thieves had broken in while my client was away. What unspeakable things had they done to Cicero? Only Cicero knew, and he would not tell. The Cat Psychologist got in the closet with him and talked softly for an hour. Cicero did not like sharing his closet with the Cat Psychologist, so reluctantly he came out. I gave the owner a few other recommendations, and soon Cicero was mixing with the group once more.

Several weeks later, my client called me again. Cicero's sister, Leonora, had taken to the closet to get attention. I had to bill for two sessions in the closet. So much for the cat in the closet — or even the Cat Psychologist in the closet!

Everyone wants his or her work to be stimulating and rewarding. I walk into a household that is in complete chaos because the family cat has a behavioral problem, and in two hours I leave knowing I have contributed a great deal. I have made the cat's life healthier and less stressful, and I have made the owners better understand their beloved pet. Everyone is happy. I cannot imagine any work more satisfying.

I talk a lot in this book about who makes an ideal cat owner, and understanding the cat and learning to compromise. To me, pop singer Whitney Houston is a model cat owner.

Once, when she flew in to Toronto for a concert, she waited at the airport for the next plane to arrive. Was she waiting for friends, relatives or even her agent? No, the world's most famous female pop star, with seven platinum records — more than any other single or group recording artist, even the Beatles — was waiting for her two cats, Misty and Marilyn, her psychological support in one of the roughest worlds of all, show business.

This talented singer is backed by a top-rate business and promotion group. Her performing schedule and the demands on her time all exact a tremendous toll, and it takes another support group, behind the scenes, to keep her — or any performer — from falling to pieces physically and mentally.

This is where her family and her cats come in. They provide the outlet away from work necessary to all superstars. Unfortunately drugs and drink are all too handy for performers, but if they can turn to animals for comfort, they will make it through. When I first heard about Whitney Houston traveling with her cats, I contacted her agent to offer my services as a feline behaviorist, for I know that traveling does not always bring out the best in cats. Since I was just then preparing for a radio show, I asked if I could have a quote from her. This is what she said about her cats:

> I am inspired by their attention. They always know what I am doing and thinking. They are sensitive to my moods, they are lovable and kind, and they do not judge if you make a mistake. I only wish that more people were like my Misty and Marilyn.

Houston understands her cats, and theirs is an ideal person-cat relationship. The loving care she provides them with offsets the problems some traveling cats might experience.

The insert with her records includes her thanks to everyone who helped make that record, right down (or up) to Misty and Marilyn. I have often said I would like to be reincarnated as a cat, but only in a nice home. I think being Whitney Houston's cat would be wonderful.

Most of us in the nineties probably can't imagine what a fast-paced life like Houston's is really like. Yet many of us live our own brand of hectic, stressful lifestyle. It is hard for us to realize how taxing all this is on our bodies and our minds. For our dear cat, of course, it is beyond understanding.

We lesser stars of the nineties also have our tabby support system, but we must now stop and take a good look at what this crazy modern mess does to our cats. And that is what my book is all about.

ONE

The Pet of the Nineties:
The Nature of Your Cat

··

AS I GO ON MY KITTY CALLS, from the luxurious condos at Toronto's Harbourfront to modest basement apartments in the suburbs, one thing is clear to me: the role the cat now plays in people's lives is vastly different from the role it played forty years ago, when I was growing up.

When I was a girl, cats were in the background of the home, taken for granted, never mistreated, free to sleep all day and go out roaming at night. Neutering and spaying, such a necessary part of our present-day cat's life, were not done — cats were whole and in their natural habitat.

Today the cat is in the forefront of the home. Whether this is good for the cat, it is what the owners want and desperately need. The cat is a substitute for poor or nonexistent human relationships; he keeps his owner in touch with nature in a world of unnatural technology; his beauty is food for your soul; and he is a dear friend who comforts you through sickness and emotional problems. Best of all he is *always there*.

But people are sometimes more strongly attached to their cats than they are to other humans. Even when owners live in a house with a large garden, they are afraid to let their cat outside for fear they may lose him. This dependence is a phenomenon of the nineties, and it is making the cat's life a living hell, cutting off his freedom of movement and his need to be close to nature.

This fear of losing the cat has made it possible for others to step in and pass bylaws in many places throughout Canada that forbid the cat from going outside unless he is on a leash. If you happen to be one of a dying breed of old-fashioned cat lovers who still believes in your cat being in his natural habitat, and your cat wanders onto your neighbor's property once too often, you can be fined. Are many of us not to be allowed to have a cat?

Of course, no cat lover would ever dream of putting their pet out to play in busy traffic. It goes without saying that whether the cat goes out is a judgment call that depends on the situation. But what is behind keeping the cat shut up indoors is not entirely worry about his being hit by a car, or getting lost or stolen or sick or whatever. (Since drink and drugs are not part of the cat's lifestyle, he's naturally at an advantage on the roads.) The plain fact of the matter is, cat owners of the nineties are frantic with worry whenever their cat ventures out, even into the garden, because they need the cat too much and would be devastated if anything happened to him.

Now, some concern is understandable, but when it reaches unnatural proportions it has to be dealt with, for the cat's sake. If the nineties cat is going to be an indoor cat, the least we can do, as responsible cat lovers, is replace the habitat the cat has lost as best we can, so he will live a long, healthy and, almost forgotten for the cat, *happy* life.

WHAT MAKES YOUR CAT TICK?

WHY DOES YOUR CAT look at you like that? Why does your cat, for no apparent reason, go crazy once a day? Why does your cat sometimes scratch near his favorite food as if he were in a litter box? Why does your cat suck, knead, meow, wag his tail? Why, why, why?

The cat, so mysterious, so misunderstood, so lucky (or unlucky, as the case may be), so soft yet hard, so independent yet loving.

In actual fact the cat is not one bit mysterious, nor is he hard to understand. The cat is just being The Cat and doing what comes naturally to him. To someone like me — indeed to millions of cat owners — nothing the cat does is weird. We understand his inner workings and *expect* him to behave the way he does. The cat is unusual only to those who do not understand him, and of course these people also number in the millions.

As I found out when I ran the Cats' Cradle, boarding hundreds of cats without cages, there are rules in the cat kingdom of which we humans know nothing at first. But if you watch and wait, the cats themselves will show you the way.

Cat Rule #1: Listen to what your cat is telling you. Be aware of what his instincts are telling him, and the two of you will get on just fine.

You can never pamper a cat too much, because deep down he knows he is one of the most beautiful and intelligent creatures in the world, and he expects to be treated accordingly. If he gets the freshest water, the freshest food, the cleanest litter box, the softest bed and is not bothered unless he asks to be, he will be a happy cat. It is a cat's nature to look for and expect these basics, and it is your duty as a responsible cat owner to see that your cat receives them. After all, you're happiest when you get what you want, too.

We have a lot to learn from the cat, such as how to have fun while exercising, that fresh food and water are best for us, that cleanliness of body is a worthwhile occupation, and how to be beautiful of spirit. For those in the dark, I will attempt to explain some cat "mysteries."

Once a day your cat will get up, stretch, then seemingly go mad. He will run along the back of the sofa, leap up the walls, race around the corners, screech to a halt, only to start his antics all over again — all of this to a cat lover's delight and a new cat owner's horror. What's going on? Simple. This is exercise and high spirits "cat style." Nature tells him he needs exercise, so he takes it and enjoys it. If only we would learn from the cat!

You serve him his favorite supper and he scratches around it the way he does in his litter box. Why is this? A new cat owner watches nervously, trying to figure out Mr. Cat. Again it's very simple. He does not like his food anymore or it isn't fresh. His wonderful nose for freshness works with his natural instinct for what he needs, and he tells you this is not it by trying to cover the food up. So cook him some economical, nutritious liver and watch him perk up. Won't that spoil him? You're darn right it will, and that's what a cat thrives on — good, sensible spoiling. And why not? You love him, he's yours for the next twenty years, and you want a healthy cat, not healthy vet bills.

Why does your cat stare at you like that? He's not really *staring* at you, he's just thinking (or not thinking, depending on how you view the cat), and you just happen to be in his line of vision. Of course, if the eye contact goes along with a meow, yes, he's probably trying to tell you something. If he's sitting in front of the fridge, you know what he wants. If he's at a closed door, you know what he wants. But sometimes, especially if you take time to talk to your cat, you may find he's just making friendly conversation.

And while we're talking about talking, do you know what an "errp" is? In my house, when our cats made little friendly noises, not meows, we called them "errps." Miss Tits, the Queen of Cats, used to say this when she was especially happy, rubbing in and out of our legs. All happy cat owners know the sound, and if you follow the directions in this book of good cat care, you will be rewarded all through your cat's life with little "errps."

I have my own special cat language, which is like baby talk and sounds silly to other people, even some cat owners. But cats love it (which is the point), and when I go to a client's house I usually talk to the cat with my "cat chat." This and the sound of my voice tell the cat I am his friend. Many times a withdrawn or shy cat will end up sitting on my lap through a session — to the surprise of his owner. And occasionally they even slip out the door while I'm saying my goodbyes and follow me to the elevator. I am the Pied Piper of cats — because I talk to them in their own language.

Don't be afraid to talk to your cat, especially if you will be away all day and he will be left on his own. Whether you talk human language or make catlike sounds, it serves to give him some attention before you leave, and he will settle down for a long, contented sleep while you are gone. Don't reject this idea as silly until you have tried it — your cat's reaction will surprise you.

In the morning, when you are getting ready for work and he follows you from place to place, talk to him quietly and cheerfully. And when you come home in the evening, tell him what you have been doing all day and ask him what he has been doing. Watch the different expressions on his face as you tell your stories. It is a good way of getting all your troubles out without having to go to a therapist. Besides, it's wonderful to have a friend who only listens!

There's another way to make your cat feel special and happy. He loves to be petted, *but* — and this is a big but — only when *he* wants it. If he comes to you and jumps on your lap, gently pet him — or stroke him, scratch his back, rub behind his ears (the two of you will discover what he likes best). If he winds in and out of your legs, pet him, rub your legs against him, do whatever you have discovered he likes.

But when he is cleaning himself, resting or watching birds, leave him alone. Take a clue from him as to when he wants loving — he'll come for it when he needs it. The more he is left unmolested and free, the calmer and gentler his nature will be. But the more he is hassled, the more irritable he will become. Physical contact is important, but keep in mind Cat Rule #2: Let your cat come to you. That is the secret with the cat: he knows what's best for him. So sit back and observe. When he jumps on your lap, pet him; when he wants down, let him go. Respect his freedom as you cherish your own.

Why does your cat knead a blanket — "make butter," as we used to call it? The cat is reverting to his happy kitten days when he was nursing on his mother, and will do this from time to time when he's contentedly purring in your lap or on his favorite cushion. It's nothing to worry about.

We know that a fast-wagging tail on a dog means friendly, but beware a fast-wagging tail on a cat, especially if accompanied by all his fur rising up to form a large bush. It spells trouble. Your cat is very angry or nervous about something. It's quite a sight, and though it doesn't happen often, to the new cat owner it can be scary. It is the cat's perfectly natural response to danger or fright, and has nothing to do with his love for you. Just remember, do *not* try to comfort or touch him. He will get over his fear or anxiety much faster if you leave him be — with the cause of his concern removed, if possible.

What your cat's tail is doing indicates many other moods and feelings. When your cat rubs against your legs, his tail may be wagging furiously, but he's just happy. A slowly wagging tail can mean indecision or sometimes mild displeasure. You'll see this if you stroke your cat without his asking you to. A tail held high is a sign of contentment. Our Miss Tits had a very full tail and usually walked with it held high and proudly. But when my son took out his cap pistols, or any other noisemakers, she would head promptly for the back door with her tail down. Like all cats, she hated noise.

Observe your cat's tail as he watches birds. It starts off with little flicks at the tip. As your cat gets more agitated and intense about bird watching, his tail starts to move a little faster, until finally it is flying back and forth with gusto.

Why does your cat purr? He will purr most often when he is content and happy, but he might also purr when he is in a situation he does not understand and feels anxious, and sometimes even when he's in pain. Most often, though, purring is a sign of a very content cat.

So much for the "weird, crazy, mysterious" cat. He is in

fact a gift nature has given us to enjoy, protect and learn from. We are very lucky to have the cat. Now we must make sure the cat is as lucky to have us.

THINKING LIKE A CAT

BECAUSE YOUR CAT appears self-sufficient and non-demanding, you might assume he needs nothing from you. When he's left in his natural habitat — outside — you're right. But if you keep him indoors, away from his natural world, you must replace what he has lost, or else your depressed and dejected cat will be wide open to illness and behavioral problems.

First of all, your cat loves you. You are the center of his universe, from the moment you feel him lightly jump on your bed, too early in the morning, for his breakfast, to his contented purring near your feet as you go to sleep at night. Although it is wonderful to have all the love the cat offers you, the relationship is two-way. You must stop and take notice of what has to be done to keep your cat happy, as well. He won't love you if you don't show him that you love him. A rich life together is simple when you understand your cat's nature and anticipate and meet his needs — in short, when you, the human, think like a cat.

Cat Rule #3: Do unto others . . . Imagine yourself locked in an apartment from Friday night through Sunday night, with no one to talk to and nothing to do. All there is to eat is dry bread and water, and the toilet doesn't flush. Sound cruel? When many cat owners go away for the weekend, they leave a plate of dry food and a bowl of lukewarm water, and Mr. Cat does not see or hear from anyone all weekend. Nor can he go out into the garden to amuse himself. When his owners come home and find a wet spot on their bed (because his litter box has not been changed), they get angry, shout at him, rub his nose in the mess (of course the cat has no idea what's going on) and eventually cart him off to the vet to be put down.

In this age of Protect the Whales, Save the Seals, Rescue the Endangered Species, the daily killing of millions of healthy cats in the world, because of real or imagined behavioral problems and because we don't take the time to understand the cat's nature, does not attract much attention. But it is a disgrace. I say getting our "cat act" together and putting the cat's world in order is long overdue. The *cat is in crisis* and we must help him — for he cannot help himself.

Just what has happened to change the cat from a laid-back, sleep-all-day, prowl-all-night loner to an anxious bedwetter? Could it be all the wonderful new money-making ways we have of turning his life into a living hell — declawing, pills, needles, grooming, shampooing, trendy but unnatural foods? Or could it be the incredible attachment we now have for the cat?

My research and Kitty Calls have shown me it is a combination of both. To begin to help the cat, we must back off and take a long look at what is happening to him in the nineties. Our cat is waiting for us eagerly and lovingly when we arrive home tired after a stressing day. He curls up with us to watch TV, comforts us when we are ill and pets us with a soft paw when we are depressed. At night he curls up on our bed, reassuring us with his warmth and his purring. He makes magic wherever he is. He makes us laugh with his never-dull antics and teaches our children (or us!) to be kind and gentle. For this and more we owe the cat so much. How can we ever repay him?

Well, in the past decade we have found several ways, but not all of them lead to a happy cat. With our lack of understanding of the cat's psychological needs, we force traumatic changes onto him so he'll adapt to *our* lifestyle (rather than us compromising). We declaw him, we keep him stuck indoors, we feed him what he won't eat naturally, we cart him off to the vet for shots and pills of everything from hormones to tranquilizers. And if the stress of this unnatural life builds up in the cat and he misbehaves once too often, back he goes to the vet to be killed. Not a very good return for the cat, who generates loads of happiness for us. We can do better, and we *must* do better. It isn't the cat who needs reorganizing and training — it's us, the owners.

YOUR CAT'S NEEDS

W HAT DO *YOU* ENJOY in life? Good food, a clean, stable home, freedom to come and go, fresh air, stimulating activity, some peace and quiet . . . Now imagine yourself not being able to eat what you choose, someone else being in charge, putting in front of you every day for the rest of your life a plate of dry food and a dish of water. Would you be happy? Would you be playful? Would your brain be stimulated? Would you look forward to your next meal? Or would you get depressed? Consider this. Cats are the original gourmets — a little of this, a little of that, fresh food only, please, and in a clean dish, if you don't mind. It is not that cats are finicky; it is that they are smart (next to monkeys, they are the smartest of animals, dogs and horses included) and know that variety is the spice of life. Nature has equipped them to know that a little of this and a little of that makes them healthy. If you want to live to a ripe old age, sound in body and mind — as I hope to — then you will have taken charge of your diet. And if you do likewise with your cat's diet, he will be right there with you, bright-eyed and perky, ready for action.

In the cat's natural habitat he uses nature's litter box. Very carefully he finds a secluded spot (for the cat loves his privacy), and when he is finished, he carefully covers up. He never uses the same spot twice. Now think of your litter box in the basement or in the back of the hall closet. When did you change it last? Has your cat had one too many "accidents" lately because his litter box has been so dirty he hasn't wanted to use it? With so many people lacking knowledge of the cat's behavior and needs, the whole process turns into a nightmare for both cat and owner, resulting in family fights, an embarrassingly smelly house and mistreatment of the cat. Vets prescribe hormones and tranquilizers; owners use water guns, rub the cat's nose in his mess, hit him, yell at him and, when patience runs out, put him to sleep. No one goes to the heart of the problem — the cat's extremely sensitive nose. Once we realize this, we understand how even a *slightly* smelly litter box is a nightmare come true for the ultraclean cat. An ounce of prevention now will be worth a pound of cure later on — and oh so many dollars!

Another basic need of the cat is to scratch, to stretch his claws and his muscles. But too often the cat must suffer so our furniture will not. With one scratching post and a little effort, needless cruelty can be spared. Declawing permanently damages the animal's nature. Many of my clients have been so convinced by their vets that declawing is perfectly okay that they are more than surprised to find their cat has a behavioral problem *because* he's declawed. (They are also surprised to find that the same person who said go ahead and declaw now has no idea what to do about the resulting litter problem — other than to get rid of the cat.)

Declawing is an easy, speedy solution for the thoughtless human. Your cat isn't going to change, any more than you'll give up stretching in the morning, but you can provide him with fun alternatives to the sofa and the rug. Just as we are beginning to question our doctors about the need for so many pills and operations, so must we question our vets about the validity of such customary practices. Please, I beg of you, for your cat's sake and your sake — *do not declaw.*

YOUR GOOD BEHAVIOR: A VELVET TOUCH

WHEN YOU BRING your little kitten home at twelve weeks, he is a complete package. He knows how to keep himself clean; he knows to eat and drink only what is fresh; he knows how to hunt (in case he ever ends up in his natural habitat on a permanent basis); and he knows

....

how to use a litter box. All in all, pretty nice for such a tiny little ball of energy. After he gets over the wildness of kittenhood, he turns into a serene, intelligent, affectionate pet, providing you have not tried to "train" him.

Of course, some cats have been trained to do a variety of tricks, but that is not why you have your cat. You want a loving cat who has not been made anxious by constant demands to perform various useless tricks, which is very much against a cat's nature.

Just as a dog needs "a boss" and a very firm hand, the cat needs "no boss" and a very velvet touch. If you know nothing else about cats, just keeping this in mind at all times will help enormously in your people-cat relations. A dog *must* be told what to do; a cat *must not*. The more you try to force your cat to do something or not do something, the more trouble you will have and the more bad-tempered you will make your cat.

Yelling, hitting or shooting water pistols are not the ways to change a cat's mind. These methods teach him only to be afraid of you. You wouldn't live with someone who always shouted at you or slapped you, and your cat shouldn't have to put up with that, either.

Cats learn instead by positive, or constructive, example. It's not enough just to stop them from doing something. You have to show them, right then, an alternative. For instance, if your cat is where you do not want him to be — say, on the bathroom vanity or under the kitchen sink — don't clap your hands and shoo him away. Gently pick him up, give him a kiss on the head, pop him in another room and show him something else he can do there. (You must know, however, that when your cat is alone in the house, all the areas you think you have taught him not to go to, he will go to, since it is in the free-spirited nature of the cat to do what moves him when it moves him. This is one of the many traits cat lovers admire in their cats.) Or if you find him scratching your favorite armchair, don't squirt him with water and shout at him. You'll only end up with a nervous wreck who prefers to live in the closet. Again, gently pick him up, say nice things to him and take him to his very own scratching post. Scratch it yourself to show him how enjoyable it is.

All this assumes you're not wasting your time trying to stop your cat from doing something that's natural to him — such as climbing up trees or onto bookcases or even scratching. It's not a matter of teaching him *not* to climb or scratch; it's a matter of letting him know *where* he can climb and scratch. *Compromise* is the operative word.

With common sense and this basic knowledge of feline behavior, you can handle your cat in a kind and intelligent way. Knowing that you are not the cat's "boss," but that the two of you are dear — and equal — companions will make your cat as sweet as nature intended him to be, and you will have a devoted friend for many, many years.

QUESTIONS AND ANSWERS

Question

Why does my new kitten behave so wildly? I just don't know what to expect next. I think there is something wrong. My last cat did not behave this way.

Answer

Each kitten's and cat's nature is different, just as yours and mine are different. Though one cat will be quiet and sedate and another highly energized, both are just fine. Know that the wild and woolly kitten will settle down in a few months. Enjoy this exuberant period and wait for the calm after the storm.

Question

I found a stray cat in the park and now I keep him indoors.
But he has a habit I do not understand. He tries to cover and
hide his food.

Answer

A cat who is forced to survive out of doors — in his natural
habitat — reverts to his outdoor ways. When you bring him
indoors, he still carries on as if he were outside, at least for a
little while.

Covering and hiding food — in this case, anyhow — is a
way of saving something for tomorrow. When the cat comes
back he can be sure there is still food. This is a natural
reaction for a cat who has been on the run. Put down small
portions that you know he will finish and he may get over
the habit in time — or he may not, depending on how long
he has had to fend for himself.

In other cases where a cat does this, it might just mean he
doesn't like the food or that the food is old or spoiled. This
is nothing to worry about. If it bothers you, put down very
small portions several times a day, and this behavior, too, will
pass.

Question

How do you teach a cat to go through a cat door when he
has not done so before?

Answer

Tie a small bell or a favorite catnip toy on the end of a string.
Put the toy and your cat on one side of the door while you
go to the other side and pull the string. Your cat will follow

the toy — right through the door. Go back and forth with the toy until your cat gets used to going in and out through the cat door.

Question

My cat likes to suck on my hand or neck. Is this all right?

Answer

If you do not mind, it does not matter. If you do mind, put her on the floor and encourage her to play with a toy or a ball. She was probably taken away from her mother too soon and is satisfying her need to suckle. If you offer more constructive playtime, this habit will pass. If you choose to allow the sucking, it may go on always.

Question

I had two cats, a seventeen-year-old male and his mother, who was eighteen. They never got along very well, and now that the male is dead the mother cat does not seem to miss him. Why did they not get along? Is it normal that she does not miss him? *I* miss him so much.

Answer

Once a kitten has reached twelve weeks and the mother has taught it all it needs to know, she is no longer concerned, for she considers the cat well launched in life. Even though they lived together all those years, the mother cat no longer knew the male was her kitten. Since they did not get along through life, the female does not miss him now that he is gone. Do not worry — it was all perfectly normal.

Question

My cat bites me when I am playing with her. I do not like it. What can I do to stop it?

Answer

When a cat bites you, know that playtime is over. It is the cat's sign that he is overexcited and has had enough. Pick your cat up, thank him for playing with you, very gently put him on the floor and go about your business. If you remember Cat Rule #2 — Let the cat come to you — and if you pet him gently and do not work him into an overexcited state, biting should not occur.

Sometimes people roughhouse with the cat, and this is bad. The cat soon learns that everything nearby is rough, and he learns to bite and scratch in self-defense. Try to discourage this in your family. When the cat draws blood, he will be the one who is blamed — and wrongly so.

Kittens, not knowing better, just like children, sometimes bite, but they only do so in play.

Question

Why does my cat growl at thunder?

Answer

I have never heard a cat growl at thunder, but I've seen some mighty scared cats during a hailstorm, when big hailstones were bouncing on the windowpanes. Your cat is growling because he is afraid or nervous. It is normal behavior. Act calm yourself and tell him everything is okay, and he will be all right.

TWO

Cats in Crisis:
Stress and Your Cat

T HE FRUSTRATION OF ACTIVITIES natural to the animal may well be the worst form of cruelty." So said the English biologist Sir John Huxley.

To say that the cat in the nineties has her natural activities taken away from her and is thereby frustrated is an enormous understatement. With the cat crisis we have on our hands today, we know that we are indeed practicing cruelty, cruelty that comes in many forms: depriving the cat of her natural habitat, feeding her poor-quality, chemical-laden foods, mutilating and constantly attacking her fragile body in the name of so-called necessity and vanity. And a final testament to our cruelty is the shocking statistic of millions of cats put down worldwide, victims of our lack of knowledge and lack of caring about what the cat needs to be happy.

I once thought all cats were as well adjusted as my Miss Tits, but I know now it was my understanding of her nature and my proper treatment of her that made her so healthy and completely free of behavioral problems. She is the yardstick by which I measure all my clients' cats. It never fails me.

She had, first of all, the number-one prerequisite for a cat's mental health — freedom of movement in her natural habitat. Our home on a quiet street in a modest suburb of Toronto had three doors, front, side and back, as well as basement and upstairs windows that were always open in the nice weather. (Back then — and it wasn't so long ago — we didn't have to worry about burglars.) Miss Tits's territory was the large front and back yards, with an occasional foray across the quiet road to visit our friend's overgrown garden and tumble-down garage full of old furniture. Miss Tits loved to pad over there on a sunny day to check out the bird situation and snooze on one of those dusty old chairs. Cats love tiny adventures, and for Miss Tits to be so far from home was enough for her.

If I went for a walk and she was accompanying me, she would soon start to meow anxiously, telling me we were now out of her territory and she could go no farther. She would then sadly go back home and turn quickly into our front yard, looking around carefully to make sure everything was just as she had left it.

She took great pride in policing her territory and was a perfect angel, quiet and refined, until anything dared put a foot on it. Dogs were run off no matter what their size. Other cats were run off if they were females, though males were sometimes allowed to stay. And squirrels were ignored — as a kitten she had learned they could walk on wires to get completely out of her reach.

So you see, for good mental health, a cat must not only have her natural habitat but must feel that her other natural instinct, protecting her territory, is also part of her day. This gives her a reason to get up every morning, and she lives a longer and healthier life.

Now, you and I both know that such an idyllic life is for hundreds of thousands of cats no longer possible. You must realize what your cat has given up for you and know what you must do to make up for these losses. To do otherwise is nothing short of cruel. In this modern age we have taken away the cat's natural habitat and replaced it with nothing.

CAT STRESS IN THE NINETIES

THE CAT IS THE PET of the nineties, and the nineties lifestyle is radically different from any other. Instead of living spread out, with lots of room for people and cats, we now move high into the sky, in apartments and condos that soar higher every year. Concrete replaces grass, and gardens, when they exist, are minuscule. As we people of the nineties become more hassled and harried by our fast-paced life, the comfort the cat gives us becomes more essential. But even the wonderful cat has her limits and slips into what has been referred to as "the gray area," where she can no longer handle the situation. This happens when the cat no longer receives what she requires to function normally, and, after a series of traumas, she develops, for example, a litter problem: she stops using her litter box and instead soils the house. Unfortunately for her, this is the very thing that will get her killed quickly by the fast-moving impatient people of the nineties — because we can't be bothered to understand her needs.

Are cat owners altogether to blame? Even though the cat has been with us for thousands of years, her behavior has never been deeply studied. Also, in times past there was not such a strong need to understand the cat, for we allowed her to act naturally in a natural environment: garden, trees, freedom, the hunt, natural food, sex life and so on. Now, in the so-called good life, we are selfishly depriving her of these things. If we take away from her everything that goes into making her the creature we love so much, we will destroy — just as we are destroying our own natural habitat — her nature. Today's cat is in crisis.

This is where I come in, as the only person in Canada going out each day to aid the cat in her nineties habitat. With my old-fashioned, natural approach to the cat (whose nature has not changed in thousands of years — only *we* have changed *our* lifestyle) I can tell you how to make up to your cat for what we humans are taking away; I can also tell you when you have gone too far and pushed her into "the gray area." A cat's stress manifests itself in many ways that are displeasing to her owners. She chews leather or wool, or becomes withdrawn or ill, bites or scratches, or develops a litter problem. If you want to avoid such behavioral or physical problems in your cat, you, as a responsible owner, must do your best to minimize the stresses in your cat's life. With my help, you will develop a new sensitivity to your cat's nature and will learn how to cut down on those stresses.

Watch your cat and you will learn very quickly that she does not like certain things — loud noises, sudden movements, too much hustle and bustle, a lot of strangers, cigarette smoke . . . basically the same things we humans dislike.

"Don't slam the door!" How often do we repeat that? Certainly we're not worried about the damage to the door. We say it because we don't like the noise. It startles us, it makes us jump and maybe it hurts our ears. Next time you're about to slam the door, think of your cat. She is not able to rationalize the way we humans can and say to herself, "Oh, it's just a door. Nothing to worry about." She is much more attuned to her instincts, and a sudden loud noise or sudden rapid movement means danger to her: her heart pounds, her adrenaline flows, her eyes widen, she is alert for enemies. You might think that because she gets over it just as quickly as you get over a little scare, it is not important. But you are wrong. It's stressful. (And it *does* hurt her sensitive ears.)

A cat who lives with constantly slamming doors, stomping adults or shrieking children is a cat enduring constant stress. If she has also lost her natural habitat and has nowhere to run but under a bed, over time the stress becomes unbearable and behavioral problems and illness arise.

If you want a well-adjusted, lively cat, you can't expect her to just get used to what she doesn't like — thumping rock music, slamming doors, a big barking dog in the house. Of course this doesn't mean you have to sell your stereo and your dog and not have children (or not have a cat till your children have left home). But it does mean you can make room for mutual adaptation. You *know* your cat, with her extrasensitive ears and her dislike of noise, will never get used to your loud music, so keep the volume a little lower. And if you — or your teenagers — feel the need to pump up the volume now and then, recognize your cat's needs. If you can't let her outside, do her a favor: pop her in a quiet room and pull the door to. Your cat will love you for it.

Recently I visited an eighty-year-old client in her high-rise apartment. Her cat had had a litter problem for nearly fifteen years, and the apartment, with broadloom wall to wall, was in a sorry state. Her vet had given the cat a clean bill of health and had no idea what to do about the behavioral problem, and my client, not wanting to get rid of her friend of all these years, got on as best she could.

During our session I tried to find out what had been happening in the cat's life to make it so upset. First of all, it had been declawed — always a bad start in life for a cat. It was also left alone for long periods, for this lady had a busy social life and was not home very much. The cat was fed only dry food and water. No wonder it was miserable. But there was something more. At one point my client wanted the cat to come to us, and instead of calling it or asking me to fetch it, she quickly reached out, grabbed it by the tail and gave it a vicious jerk towards her. As I gasped she hoisted the protesting and snarling cat onto her lap — by its tail!

Without even thinking I shouted, "You can't do that!" She shouted back, "And why not? I've been doing it for fifteen years!"

After I had calmed down, I explained to her that cats do not like that sort of cruel treatment — which, by the way, she did not think was cruel, but only a method to catch her cat. I told her that not only could she injure her cat physically, but she was keeping the cat in a constant state of anxiety because it never knew when it might next have this pain inflicted. The stress caused by this tail pulling had clearly been a major factor in the cat's longstanding litter problem.

I provided the owner with my list of instructions on diet and exercise, beginning with *Never pull a cat by its tail*, and her cat is now leading a more comfortable and happy life. The apartment smells fresh again, too!

That's just one example of the hundreds of ways we inflict

harmful stress on our cats without always realizing it. And it needn't be something as obvious as pulling tails. This client's cat also had the stresses of poor and boring diet, loneliness and lack of exercise.

The elimination of what disturbs us in life makes us calmer, healthier and more pleasant to be with. Likewise your cat. Remember Cat Rule #3, Do unto others . . . ? The elimination from this cat's life of pain, boredom and lethargy led to a calmer, healthier and more-pleasant-to-be-with cat — and a happy owner.

It's a fact of modern urban life that if we are going to have cats living with us indoors only, we will be depriving them of much that they naturally expect — birds to eat, grass to roll in, trees to scratch and climb. The best way to stop feeling guilty about your friend's loss of habitat is to do something about it. Once you know you have done the best you can for your cat, then you are happy and your cat is happy. After all, in this frazzling world humans are not exactly living a natural lifestyle, either. Compromises must be made both ways. Just remember, always, that if you take away something your cat requires, you *must* provide a replacement.

Consider food, for example. For a cat who goes outside and does catch the odd mouse or bird and eats grass and insects, perhaps the lack of good food is not quite as hard on him as on the indoor cat, who has lost her natural diet completely (to say nothing of fresh air and sunshine).

Often the indoor cat does not see anyone for hours, sometimes days, on end. In these cases food is not only important but almost the only pleasure the cat has to look forward to. And what does she get? Dry whatever-it-is and a bowl of water, same old thing day after day. It's no surprise that this leads to boredom, which leads, as it does in humans, to depression, which leads to physical illness and behavioral problems. We must do better than this. We must provide the most healthy and natural meals for our cats. (I discuss diet in detail in chapter 4.)

Depriving our cats of a natural, wholesome, varied diet may seem minor compared to some of the other things we do to them to make them — or so we believe — happily fit in with our modern lifestyle:

We remove claws and claw bed.

Trauma of surgery
- Pain for three days
- Caged at vet's
- Can't exercise in the same way, so muscles atrophy
- Stress of being defenseless

We overvet, constantly taking them for shots and pills from hormones to tranquilizers, for treatments from acupuncture to dental work to shampoos and blow-drying.

Trauma of being restrained and in pain

We shut front and back doors so they will never get out.

Trauma of being deprived of their natural habitat

We clean their litter boxes once a week *if* they are lucky.

Trauma of having an innate need for cleanliness and privacy denied

We leave them alone at nights, all weekend and on holidays.

Trauma of loneliness, boredom and isolation

We put them in harnesses and on leashes and try to walk them like dogs.

Trauma of being robbed of freedom

All these things are either unnecessary or, with a little care and common sense, avoidable. Let me go through this list of traumas one by one.

DECLAWING

I'VE ALREADY TALKED about declawing in chapter 1. In a word, *don't*. If your cat is already declawed, though, first of all stop feeling guilty. What's done is done, and there is no going back *with this* cat. Though your cat has already experienced her most major trauma, if you cut out as many future traumas as you can, in time she will become more relaxed, less anxious and will learn to trust you again.

Keeping your declawed cat physically and mentally healthy will mean very few trips to the vet, where she was subjected to this trauma in the first place. As important, give your declawed cat a reason to live. Surprise her with a new food: a tasty bit of meat from the roast, cooked chicken livers, a dish of warm milk or some cooked fish. If money is short, just give her some cooked hamburger with a few pieces of lettuce and a little pasta or potato. A hungry, healthy cat will love it. Surprise her with a fresh catnip mouse, a new soft ball (inexpensive), a brown paper bag, a carton or the cardboard from the toilet tissue roll. Just like little children, cats would rather play with the wrappings than the expensive toy. Stroke her softly and talk quietly to her. Play my hide-and-seek game (from chapter 4's section "Play and Exercise") and throw the ball for her. In other words, it's back to Cat Rule #3: Do unto others . . .

OVERVETTING

WHEN DO YOU SAY NO to drugs for your cat in this world of pill pushing for us as well as our pets?

Again I'll use Miss Tits as an example of the natural and healthy cat. In her many long years she was sick just once. I took her to the vet, who said that she had tonsillitis and that he had never seen it before in a cat. Other than when she was spayed I never had to take her to the vet again, for anything. She did not even have her shots.

Recently I was interviewed by a young man who said he and his family had had their cat for years. Their cat had lived as my Miss Tits had: with easy access to his habitat, natural, fresh food (never commercial cat food), and, like Miss Tits, his cat did not go for shots and had never been sick a day in his life. He was now eighteen years old and going strong. I have heard similar stories many times.

Vets who read this will say I am setting back veterinary medicine with this type of chat. But we are now entering a new era in our understanding of and our approach to how to keep ourselves healthy and how much doctoring (in this case vetting) is really necessary. We are technically progressing ourselves and our cats to death, physically with environmental pollution and mentally with stress and drugs (prescribed and otherwise). Just as we in North America have become the biggest pill and drug takers in the world, we have inflicted this practice on our cats. Two out of three of my clients' cats have been prescribed tranquilizers.

Tranquilizers never solve behavioral problems. Instead, good *preventive* medicine must be practiced: fresh air and exercise, fresh food, human company for your cat, spaying/neutering, no declawing — all will keep your cat mentally and physically healthy.

THE SHUT-IN CAT

ONE OF THE WAYS humans work off stress is by exercising. And to work off the stress that builds for your indoor cat, you must work some exercise into her routine. There are many ways you can do this and I suggest some in chapter 4, but the main thing is to *do something every day*. Once you start your new cat care routine aimed at preventing illness, it will be perfectly natural for you to toss a ball, play hide-and-seek, put down a new carton or brown paper bag or throw the empty toilet tissue roll on the floor.

In these simple ways, you will bring indoors the excitement your cat gets outdoors, where everything is thrilling for her. The whisper of a leaf, the chirping of a cricket, a bird warbling in the branches — these all stir up the natural juices of your cat. Stalking a bird stimulates the instincts of the cat, giving her an appetite and putting her in a joyous, playful mood.

Unfortunately lifestyles in the nineties have taken all that away. So, you cat owner in your condo or apartment, follow my advice about exercise and play and get those juices flowing in your cat. You will see a change in attitude *and* promote good health.

THE DIRTY LITTER BOX

T HIS I'VE TALKED ABOUT, and I discuss it in depth in chapter 4. Remember, cats like it clean, please. Do you like to use a toilet that hasn't been flushed?

LONELINESS

I FEEL SO GUILTY about leaving my cat I never go on holiday." I so often hear this statement from cat owners, and it is a sentiment I can quite understand. Such people are overly anxious; they are so attached to their cats that they cannot enjoy themselves if their pet is not there with them. So they never stay out late and they never take holidays. This is not healthy for the cat owner. On the other side of the coin are the cat owners who work late into the night, go away on weekends and holidays two or three times a year, too often neglecting their cat.

These two extremes of cat owners are the ones I see most often. The first are too hard on themselves; the second are too hard on their cats. A happy medium must be found.

To begin with, my questions in chapter 3 will tell you whether you are cut out to be a cat owner. I hope these questions will reduce the number of people who should never bring a cat into their current lifestyles. Put simply, if you're away every weekend and out working or socializing most nights of the week, you shouldn't have a cat. You will only be making her life miserable.

Remember that you are the center of your cat's world, and she depends on you for comfort and support. When you do not return day after day, it is very hard on her.

I believe that as long as you are kind to your cat in the most necessary ways, taking a vacation — or a business trip — is not something you should feel guilty or anxious about. To minimize your cat's stress (and your own worries) when you go away — whether for a few days or several weeks — two considerations reign supreme. First, your cat has to have human contact. Someone must come and visit her at least once a day to feed her, stroke her, play with her, clean her litter box. Second, always choose home over a kennel or boarding your cat at the vet's. Cats hate change and love to be in their own homes, on familiar territory. Boarding is too stressful, with its change in environment, diet, routines, with the strange-smelling strangers and the noises and odors of other cats.

These days most urban centers have cat- and house-sitters who can come into your home a couple of times a day or overnight to look after your cat as you would. Make sure the company you choose is bonded and that a friend has already used its services and been satisfied.

If you are trying pet-sitters for the first time, go away just for a night or two and see how it works out. Buy a new toy, leave favorite foods and give lots of extra love before you go and when you come back (I'm sure I don't have to tell you this). You may be surprised to discover that your cat gets on just fine if the pet-sitter is truly a cat lover and takes time to play with and pamper your cat.

You might also ask a friend, relative or neighbor to drop by a couple of times a day or, if you're away for more than a few days, to stay in your house. Just make sure you know your house-sitter. I have seen many cases where a quiet household has been drastically changed. People who go on holiday and let friends come in and look after their cat have come back to some unpleasant surprises. Very often the cat-sitters have partied, with music blaring and many people coming and going. A cat used to a quiet house for many years is terrorized by all this unusual behavior. When the owners arrive home, I am often called in to determine what has happened to their normally well-behaved cat. After much detective work, I can always explain to the cat's owners where things took a wrong turn.

As you grow more relaxed about being away, plan a week's holiday, and when all is well, go for the big vacation, with the house-sitter staying in your home while you are off enjoying a worry-free break.

LEASHES AND CAT BYLAWS

OTTAWA, THE CAPITAL CITY of Canada, has a terrible problem — cats are walking free. During their quiet strolls what are the cats doing? Biting people? No. Leaving deposits for people to step in? No. Stealing from stores? No. Frightening children? No. They are just being free. Strolling across people's lawns or along back fences, stopping to investigate and, from time to time, leaving their footprints on people's cars.

This "problem" was brought to my attention by Hilary Mackay, vice-president of Pet Owners United in Nepean, a city near Ottawa. She told me a bylaw had been passed whereby a cat who walks into a neighbor's garden once too often and is, as they say, "left unattended," can be reported. The owner is supposed to be warned, and if it happens again the cat will be picked up (or trapped) by the animal control people and held until someone comes to bail it out. This will cost you $28.50 plus daily expenses. If you do not get there in time, your cat will be put up for adoption, sold for animal research or killed. Of twenty cats already trapped, twelve were killed by the Humane Society, the others claimed by their owners or adopted. Two other suburbs have also set up this bylaw, and similar plans are being considered in towns and cities across Canada.

I have received copies of all the newspaper articles from Ottawa covering this new stress for cats, and they are all with one voice on the side of the cat. In Nepean the effects of this foolish bylaw are now being felt not only by the poor cats but by the people: a man put his cat on a leash for the first time so it would not get picked up because of the bylaw and his cat strangled to death.

What a sorry state of affairs. With so many more important issues to put our energies into, such as cleaning up the environment, halting our drug epidemic and solving poverty, hunger and the lack of housing, we now have a group of people whose lives are devoted to keeping cats from walking through our gardens.

I personally am going to fight to have such bylaws revoked where they have already been passed and will make sure that they are not passed elsewhere. If any of my readers hears of a city, town or suburb considering this bylaw, please let me know (my address is at the back of this book).

I cannot begin to tell you how cruel it is to tie up a cat, either with a rope, a leash or a harness. The cat's nature is to be free, and to go against that is the ultimate cruelty. Leashing *must* be stopped.

All these stresses are, as I said, unnecessary or avoidable. Yet our cats are also subject to many stresses that can't be avoided. Moving houses, for example, is upsetting to your cat, but no one can reasonably expect you to stay put in the same house or apartment for as long as you have your cat. The key with the following unavoidable stresses is helping your cat cope as best she can.

Spaying and Neutering

NOT ON MY LIST of things not to do to cats are spaying and neutering, still traumatic but nonetheless necessary. Both produce a loss of sex life, and in the female, a stifling of the motherhood instinct. Yet just as surgery is stressful for us, sometimes it has to be done, and spaying/neutering is a fact of modern life. Being an attentive and understanding owner can make the stresses much easier for your cat to bear.

Never during my research or in any discussion with cat owners have I heard anyone say we are taking from the cat when we have it spayed or neutered. We feel that if we humans say it is all right, then it must be so. But any time we take something away from a cat, it is less a cat.

Since I am going to start up free spay/neuter clinics for people who cannot afford the service, you must know that I believe in the need for it to be done. But it is important to the cat owner (and the about-to-be cat owner) to understand that the added stresses of declawing, poor diet, no exercise and loss of habitat are far too much for any cat to bear. We cannot cope with the cat population that we have, so we must prevent the production of unwanted kittens. Both male and female cats, neutered or spayed in a kind, understanding way and nursed with tenderness, do not show behavioral problems. Males, especially, become much more affectionate and more housebound. *But* — and this is a big but — spaying/neutering is the only major trauma we should put our cat through in order to help it fit into our lifestyle. Any added trauma is nothing short of cat abuse.

Chaotic Environments

THE CAT HAS AN INSTINCTIVE need for stability, order and routine. If you move one chair in your living room or bring in a new piece of furniture, it can upset your cat. Depending on how well adjusted she is, she may or may not spray the new furniture or be anxious until she gets used to the rearrangement, but you must always keep in mind that even a minor change can upset her. So you can understand what is happening to the cats of the nineties with our constant changes in everything from houses to families to lifestyles.

The fast-paced people of the nineties work all day, play all night and take off for the weekends. Where does this leave the cat? Sure, she can and does have a little case of the fits every day and chases her tail, but the same old game soon gets boring, even for the enterprising cat — just as the same old thing bores you. There are no two ways about it. A cat owner who's away at the office twelve hours a day, stays out for dinner, comes home late, watches TV for half an hour and collapses into bed — well, a person who leads a life like this can't expect the family cat to be well adjusted. Depression sets in over her lack of people contact, her lack of natural habitat and her lack of mental stimulation, and illness and psychological problems predictably follow. Now is this the cat's fault or the owner's?

When the fast-paced people of the nineties aren't working or playing, they're often breaking up old and entering new relationships. As I make my Kitty Calls, I encounter relationships that are new and different and still rapidly changing. Father and Mother are working, children are at daycare or with nannies, and all sorts of new people are coming and going, not only in the family's life but in the family cat's life, too. A live-in lover, his children, her children, her dogs, his cats, a divorce settlement that includes "who gets the cat." Life in the nineties is fast, confusing and full of stress. Relationships and families are undergoing unprecedented changes, and lots of things are being caught in the crossfire. One of these is the family cat.

Change, however painful, is necessary, and it cannot be avoided. But since your cat is innocent and not able to fend

for herself in the midst of all these upheavals, you need to
know how to make things easier for her. In the face of all
these momentous changes, it's easy to ignore your pet's
needs and say, "Oh, it's just a cat." But your cat is part of
your family, and when your family goes through change so
does your family cat. Make time to listen to her, and know
that if something is upsetting or stressing you, chances are
it's upsetting or stressing her, too.

But remember Cat Rule #2: Let her come to you. Don't
rush her. Let her take things at her own pace. When she has
calmed down over the move to a new house, the strange man
in her bed, the strange woman at the breakfast table, the new
children making all that noise or the new baby, she will come
back to you. That's what true friends are all about.

MOVING BLUES —
THE VALUE OF THE SPECIAL ROOM

WHEN IT'S TIME TO MOVE OUT, or move in with
someone new (or even if your relationship is perfect
and you're just moving), you must remember that
your cat hates change of any kind. Even when you move her
favorite chair, she is not thrilled, so when you pick up the
whole household every year or two, maybe leave old family
behind and add new family, your cat becomes especially
disoriented and stressed.

You can best help your cat cope with the confusion of
moving by first establishing a room in the new living quarters
as *her* special room. Whenever I mention the "special room"
for your cat to recover in or just be when you are moving to
new quarters, I do not mean it has to be a spare room in the
house; not all of us have spare rooms we can turn over for
the exclusive use of a cat. The special room can be any room
where your cat can be free of the stress of the household.
This may be the bathroom, or a bedroom when no one is in
there. It is not meant as punishment. It is meant as a place

of solitude and safety. When you establish this special room, put in a cardboard box with her favorite blanket or cushion, a clean litter box, food and water, shut the door and get on with your moving. Because it's the cat's nature to roam and check up on what's happening, she might not enjoy being confined to one room. No matter how comfortable her bed is or how much fun her toys are, she'll scratch at the door and call you. Stop by often and play with her, hug her, talk to her and feed her. This way you will not only keep your cat happy, you will know where she is and not always worry about her getting underfoot or getting outside in a strange area. (If this happens too soon, she could very easily go looking for her old home, and you might never see her again.)

When you are completely moved in, let her out of her room to inspect and put her scent around her new territory. She does this by rubbing against, over and under everything, and you might not even realize she's doing it.

Do not forget to clean her litter box every day, or she might establish her territory in a way you will not like — urinating in the new house, a favorite trick of disoriented cats.

If your cat is going to be an outdoor cat, keep her inside for at least two weeks until she gets used to the house. Then "butter her paws." The idea here is that a little butter on your cat's front paws, needing to be licked off, will make her feel that she is indeed home. Maybe, also, butter being such a nice treat for her, she will not wander too far from the house that gave it to her. Anyway, "butter her paws," and when she starts to go out, go with her for short periods at a time, reassuring her and telling her she's safe. Little by little increase the time until she feels at home in her natural habitat, coming indoors when she wishes and going out when she wishes.

If you follow this routine every time you move, you will

cut down on your cat's anxiety, eliminate behavioral problems and keep your cat as happy as you can, under the
circumstances.

Moving into a home that already has other people in it is an
added strain on your cat. New people should be introduced
slowly.

The new people you will be living with will probably want
to scoop up and hug the beautiful new cat that has just
arrived. Discourage this. The last thing your cat wants when
her whole life has been turned upside down is to have a
stranger pick her up. She may be nervous and lash out at the
new person, starting off in a bad way right from the beginning. Just as people relationships should move slowly and
surely, so should new people-cat relationships. To stand back
and say "My, what a lovely cat" is good enough until you are
all better acquainted.

When I am on my Kitty Calls I never touch a cat until it
comes to me. I never pick up my clients' cats; this is the first
time they have ever seen me, and it would put them in a state
of panic to have me scoop them up and bother them. Because
I leave them alone (Cat Rule #2: Let her come to you), in
almost 99 percent of cases these cats always come out to see
me without my having to hunt them down, and many of
them end up on my lap, beside me or lying on my notebook
as I am trying to take notes. They sense by how I behave that
I am their friend and can be trusted.

It never hurts to let the new people feed your cat from
time to time and gently play with her with a ball or a pull
toy — never in a rough or play-fight manner.

If you and your cat are moving into a home that is already
another cat's territory, your cat suffers further stress. Her
instincts tell her that it's dangerous to trespass on another
cat's territory, and she panics when she realizes that she can't
get away and establish her own territory somewhere.

Again the "special room" approach is most effective for helping your cat cope with these strains. Never bring your cat to her new home and throw her right in the path of the cat who lives there. Instead, put your cat in her special room, which you have arranged with a nice cardboard carton, with a cozy blanket inside, and food, water and litter nearby, and let her get used to that room only. A few days later, open the door and let her investigate one room at a time. Allow the established cat to come sniffing around. Keep your eye on the cats when they meet, but from a distance. They have their own cat ways of working things out, so supervision without too much interference will work the best. If there's any sign of trouble, put your cat immediately back in her room and try again the next day. You know there is no hurry, since you are going to have your pet for the next twenty years, so a few days will not make much difference. Even with the door closed, the cats can smell each other, and this alone gets them used to each other's presence. Often animals mix well right from the start, but sometimes they take a little longer, depending on whether you rush them or not. Do not leave the cats alone together until you are sure they are friends.

This "special room" method works in a number of situations — introducing cat to cat, kitten to older cat or cat to dog. Always, patience is the key to success. It may take hours, days or weeks, depending on the animals and how you handle the transition.

And remember, the established cat should be made the most fuss over, as too much fussing over that new arrival is a sure way to upset the older resident.

So, you nineties people, get on with your reassessment of relationships, and keep your cats, but remember my common-sense "special room" advice as you make each move, and you and your cats will be much happier.

DOMESTIC DISPUTES

HER ARM WAS IN A CAST and her cat was spraying the drapes. We were an hour into the conversation before I found out she was being beaten up regularly by her husband. Her cat was her life and her comfort during the long and horrifying marriage. When she called me to find out why her cat was spraying her drapes, it never occurred to her that the pain she was feeling was also being felt by him. Confused, anxious and frightened of the loud violent noises, his beloved mistress crying and screaming, her cat went straight to the drapes and sprayed.

When the truth came out during our session, I was alerted to a new kind of feline psychological abuse, and I have recognized it many times since. I carry with me hotline phone numbers where the victims of wife beating can get professional help, but what about their cats?

My cat of many years, Miss Tits, always came to me when I cried, very anxious and very comforting, patting me on the cheek with her soft paw. When I yelled at my son to stop climbing trees in our back yard, Miss Tits would be hanging on my ankle, telling me to stop that noise. What she would have done under drastic circumstances, such as a beating, I do not know.

Although the case of this one woman is an extreme (but common) one, cats by nature are sensitive and are easily upset by even small family arguments or children squabbling. It doesn't take much to stress the cat, and steps must be taken to protect her as much as we can. I admit it's extremely hard for anyone going through a trauma — whether raised voices at the dinner table or a wife beating — to think of their cat, but I would suggest that if you see trouble coming, put your cat outside or in another room and pull the door to. You are going to need your cat to help get you through the coming hard times, and if you put her through too much she will start to spray, and maybe then you won't have her with you when you need her most — spraying in a tense household usually leads to the cat's being put to sleep.

TOBACCO SMOKE

MY CLIENT HAD TWO CATS and the number-one people-killer of all the addictions — nicotine. Our first contact was by mail, when I received from him a long, detailed letter about his cats and their diet. Both cats had poor coats with patches of hair falling out. This man had a great love for his dear cats. Fearing that tinned and dry food were not giving them all they needed, he was supplementing their diet with all sorts of pills and powders. None of this was making any difference, so he asked me to come and advise him.

When he opened the door of his apartment I knew that this was the home of a smoker. The nasty smell hit me straight away, before I had even seen the overflowing ashtrays. As we sat down he lit up, and we were off for two hours of misery for me and for those two cats.

The apartment was not large, and because he ran a business from his home, the room was piled high with papers and all sorts of office equipment. The phone rang, the fax machine blared, the typewriter would go into action any minute. It was a nightmare of sound and smell, and those poor cats spent their lives there and never got outside. No wonder they were losing their hair, not to mention their sanity.

Experience has taught me several things: you cannot ask a smoker not to smoke in his own home; you cannot persuade a smoker to quit; men do not like women telling them what to do. I knew I was beat before I started on that subject, so I didn't mention the smoke to this man. I recommended he try his cats out on my natural diet (see chapter 4). At least they would enjoy their food for a change, and the nutrition would do them some good. It was a start.

Tobacco smoke, fresh or stale, assaults a cat's sensitive nose. Watch how your cat moves away when you light up. Cats are also highly susceptible to upper respiratory infections, and smoke-filled air only adds to the possibility of such infections developing — meaning expensive trips to the vet. Keep in mind that any *physical* stress heightens the cat's mental stress, which in turn causes further physical problems. Keep in mind, too, that tobacco isn't the only culprit. One marijuana joint contains as much toxicity as twenty cigarettes. The multitudes of smokers, and their cats, are in serious trouble.

So far no studies have been done on the relation of second-hand smoke to a cat's health, but it's reasonable to assume that if it is bad for us large-framed animals, it most certainly must be harmful to the delicate cat. I am sure future studies will prove this is so.

In the meantime, I offer some hints for cat owners who can't (for now) give up smoking.

If your cat never goes outside, as the two I was visiting did not, before you light up, please put your cat in a smoke-free room. She will really be grateful to you for it. If your cat goes outside every day, the danger to her physical and emotional health is already greatly, but not completely, reduced.

If you are having a party or even just having more smoking friends over, give your *best* friend a break — put her in that smoke-free room. The smoke and the noise combined will be highly stressful and may, if inflicted frequently enough, lead to a behavioral problem.

Clean air is a crucial ingredient to a healthy life for humans and cats alike. Whether you smoke now or have never smoked, if you can avoid the traps I know are there for you and your cat, you will both have a better quality of life and a longer life together.

CASE STUDIES

T HE FOLLOWING CASE STUDIES show how owners unintentionally subject their cats to stress and how that stress manifests itself as behavioral problems.

A Litter Problem

Here's the case of two cats in crisis whose salvation lay just beyond the patio doors.

This housecall was in an elegant part of town, with quiet winding roads, enormous grounds and mature trees giving a natural parklike setting. It seemed the perfect habitat for cats. I located my client's house, watching carefully for the Doberman she said she had just bought. I am afraid of most large dogs, and I had asked her to please keep the dog under control. She said she would, but I was still nervous. Sure enough, as I carefully walked up the long walk I heard the dog's low growls and barks.

My client, a lawyer, appeared at the door, held the dog and ushered me in. We immediately went to look at her lovely but overweight cats, who were huddling in the back hall, obviously under stress. They were scared to death, and I knew why. Neither these cats nor I was happy with the new acquisition, the Doberman that had been bought to protect the property. The two cats were both about three years old and were very attached to each other. One had developed a litter problem about a year earlier, and now the other was following suit. I asked some questions and glanced around. Things did not look good for the life of these two cats.

Our session was constantly interrupted by phone calls and my client's young children. I found out that the cats were never allowed outside and that their diet was the same expensive cat food day in and day out, with dry food left down all the time. With no exercise and nibbling all day, it was small wonder they were so fat.

In the short time they had lived in the house they had

established their territory, completely leaving out the busiest, noisiest areas, which were much too stressful for them. Now they had to get past the dog to get to their favorite spots, and they could not. As a result, they were staying in the kitchen and down in the basement. This with the world's most beautiful garden on a street with scarcely any traffic. And the most shocking part was yet to be revealed.

I always do a tour of the houses I visit, mainly to see what the cat's lifestyle is and to feel the ambiance, which tells me a lot about the stress the cat might be undergoing. We went down into the large basement, where it was soon obvious by the odor what I was about to discover. Opening the door to the room where the litter boxes were kept, the lawyer told me that changing them was not her job but her husband's or the cleaning lady's.

The smell was so bad I took a step back before entering one of the dirtiest rooms I have ever seen. The litter boxes were overflowing with urine and feces, and I had to get out quickly, partly because I was overcome and partly because I was so angry. How could anyone let this go on? Well, let me tell you, my Kitty Calls have shown me that litter-box neglect is epidemic.

When a cat has been traumatized by loss of habitat, overvetting, declawing, unnatural food that leads to feline urinary syndrome and other urinary and bowel problems, which in turn lead to hospitalization and pills and needles, a dirty litter box is the last straw. Her complete cat nature has been taken away. Her world, as she feels it, has gone into chaos, and she can no longer function as a cat. She loses all control of where to do what.

In all fairness to my clients, in no way do they mean to be cruel to their cats. They love them and want only the best for them. This client's fear of letting her cats outside is part of the anxiety and paranoia we now live with every day. If we as big people cannot cope with our overindustrialized world, how can we expect our cats to go out there and cope? If your spayed/neutered cat is let out in a quiet back yard on a not-too-busy street, she will have a less stressful life than you and I. She will hardly ever need to go to the vet and will be as she should be, part of your household in her *own cat way.* She will not be a stressed-out, urinating vegetable with a short lifespan.

So please, open that door for your cat's sake. If the circumstances are right, buy her an elastic collar with a nametag and then just watch your cat's joy.

As for the dirty litter box, clean up your act, or both you and your beloved cat will end up in a serious situation.

Stress of Traveling

Although a litter problem is by far the most prevalent behavior problem, stress affects cats in many different ways. Since moving from the United States to her new home in Toronto, Serena, a beautiful Persian, had developed a taste for leather: slippers, handbags, wallets, you name it. If it was leather it soon disappeared. When a guest's handbag fell victim, I was called in to see if I could help.

When we sat down for our session, the source of Serena's stress soon came out. She was a burned-out jet-setter. Apparently her owners' business had frequently taken them all over the States. Each time, they tried to find an airline that would let Serena sit up front with them, but it became harder and harder. When they learned that they would be transferred to Toronto for a year, they thought of a wonderful way to make Serena's trip more comfortable. They would hire an airplane just for Serena and themselves.

But was a leather-mad cat how they were to be repaid for their efforts — losing all their leather goods, never mind the vet bills for upset stomachs? This was clearly a case of anxiety on the cat's part (the vet had given her a clean bill of health). She had moved and moved until she did not know where she was. I knew exactly what to do.

I chose a lovely room in their beautiful home to be

Serena's "special room." I put in it her clean litter box, fresh food and water, all her favorite toys and her scratching post and, of course, nothing made of leather. Here she would be when her owners went out or had company, away from all the stress and strain of daily life. This would sharply cut down on all her anxiety.

I instructed her owners to put all their leather goods under lock and key until Serena had had time to forget her bad habit and relax in her calm new surroundings. Also, I suggested they give her lots of love and affection and playtime in her room.

All my clients call me back with reports, and I have heard from Serena's owners that she is spending less and less time in her room and walks past leather purses with disdain. Serena, befitting her name, is now serene.

Stress of Neighborhood Cats

This case is a good example of stress that has nothing to do with the owners.

Jason and Henrietta were a content old "married" Siamese couple, doted on by their loving owners. One day, without any obvious reason, Henrietta attacked Jason and left him terrified and skulking around the house, hoping she would not do this again. After a few more attacks by Henrietta, and with Jason a mere shadow of his former outgoing self, the owners called me for help. The husband had taken to sleeping downstairs with Jason and his wife upstairs with Henrietta so that war would not start in the night.

During our session I found out that neighborhood cats were coming to the doors and windows, spraying, and infringing on Jason and Henrietta's territory. This made Henrietta nervous. Not knowing what to do with that extra tension, and since cats rarely take it out on their owners, she did what most "wives" would do — she took it out on Jason.

I told my clients to discourage cats from coming on their

property by frequently soaking both the front and back yards with the hose. This would make the ground soggy and muddy underfoot, not liked by cats. I also instructed them to wash their front and back doors and all windowsills with strong soap and water and to spray those areas with a cheap heavy perfume to cover up the scent of the visiting cats with another hated smell. As well, I had them put their cats upstairs for a short time, especially when they were not home during the day to referee the proceedings, so that indoor and outdoor cats could not see, hear or smell one another. Eventually the visiting cats had no reason to come around, and the tension was gone for Henrietta. I also separated the cat couple for a little while so they would miss each other. In no time at all the house was in order again.

Stress of Lack of Space

My client earned her living by knitting at home. She had four Siamese cats, all indoor, and had just purchased a pit bull terrier, which she hoped to start on a breeding program.

Having a new dog in her small house, along with so many cats, promoted severe anxiety in one cat, who to comfort himself began to chew holes in the woman's newly created wool goods. After trying everything, she had decided to place the cat in a good home. But first she called me; she wanted me to help in the decision and get her over this painful period.

Although I would have liked to see her get rid of the dog, I had to be fair to my client. She very much wanted to go into dog breeding. If the cat could be found a good home and she could bear the loss, I could not see anything wrong with that course.

She found an excellent home, but laid down one stipulation: if she could not get over the loss, the cat must be given back. The new owner agreed. After a few weeks my client could not bear it. She asked for and got her cat back and decided to find a new home for her dog. Her wool goods are now intact and she and her cats are one happy family.

Often too many animals in a small space is not healthy. Cats require a large area to be happy. Think carefully before you take on too many animals.

Stress of Moving

My client, who had four cats, moved to a new home one mile away. One cat kept going back to the old house, and the family would have to go and search for him.

Each cat reacted to the move in a different manner, just as we humans would. Three obviously adjusted well, and one anxious cat did not.

From the story the client told me, she did not keep the cats in their new house long enough, just a few days, and when they asked to go out she let them. They seemed to be doing all right until a few weeks after they moved in, when the one went missing. I suggested that she apply my "special room" technique to enable the cat to get a good sense of the new house being *his*. Love and affection were reinforced with food treats in his own little room, lots of playtime and more attention paid to him by the family.

After a few days in the room, with lots of visiting by his owners, he was let out to mix. No matter how much he wanted to go outside he was now to be kept indoors for about three months. Then he would be let out for short periods and under supervision only. He was never to be left out overnight or all day when my clients were at work.

Eventually he forgot about his other home and the bonding was established with his new one. If by chance he ever does disappear again, the whole routine will be repeated, only for longer periods.

Stress of Teasing

Susie was declawed, left alone most evenings, had a bad, boring diet and was teased by her owner's visiting friend. The result was, she stopped using her litter box. The vet said she was a "dirty" cat and should be put down.

I explained to my caring client that she was abusing her cat without knowing it and that her boyfriend could not be allowed even to go near the cat for a long time. We established her cat's special room for when company came, put her on a natural diet, allowed for more time with her owner in the evenings and *no more teasing*. The result was a complete turnaround in the litter department, though it will be a long time before Susie learns to trust a man again.

Stressful Punishments

My client fed her kitten with an eye-dropper after its mother died while giving birth. She was declawed at an early age, ate only dry food and was left alone a great deal.

The client's husband does not like animals and says they should be disciplined, so when the little kitten bit his hand, as kittens will, especially when they have not had any training by their mother, he would hit her. As fast as she bit, he would hit, and this went on and on, until the cat was mad and bit everything that came near her. She would even jump at people's legs and hang on and bite.

The vet prescribed tranquilizers, and the fight to get the pills into the kitten was a mess of biting and hitting.

A cat never bites or scratches without a good reason, and it never takes me long to find out what has been going on. In this case the cat got off to a bad start with having no mother, and although she lived through it she was shaky and could not endure the traumas she was exposed to. She should never have been declawed, and the severe discipline she received for a normal, playful kitten set some bad habits in motion that were difficult but not impossible to cure.

I explained everything to the owner as I saw it. She was receptive to my explanations of why her kitten was biting and said she would do anything to help. I told her that her husband had to stop punishing the kitten and not even go near her for a long time. She said he was away a lot and it would be no problem to talk to him. I had to hope for the best.

A change in diet, kind treatment and more time with the kitten did, over a long time, turn the cat around. Whenever she started biting, she was put gently into another room to cool off, and was never out when company or children arrived. Of course, the pills were stopped, since tranquilizers did not change the fact that the cat was being abused.

Territorial Stresses

These clients were successful commercial artists, and their paintings and books were being badly sprayed by a very anxious male cat. Though the vet had prescribed tranquilizers, the spraying was getting worse and worse.

During our session the usual pattern emerged: the cat had been found as a stray downtown and force-fed to save his life. This made for an anxious cat who would be very easily pushed over the edge if treated incorrectly. A diet of only dry food brought on urinary problems, which led to forcing medications. A large, busy household (the litter box was out in the open) made for more anxiety, and the people, being animal lovers, encouraged any and all neighborhood cats to come into the house. Although he was an outdoor cat, his immediate territory was being threatened. (Of course he had been declawed. This is always part of the picture.) His anxiety turned into a spraying problem, and the paintings were in big trouble.

I explained to my clients that all strange cats and other animals had to be kept out of the house so their cat's territory would not be threatened. The diet had to be changed to follow my natural approach. No more tranquilizers, which would do no good, were to be administered. A clean litter box was to be put in a private place. The cat also needed to be left quietly in his special room for a time to get back into shape.

Stress of Boredom and Loneliness

My client was a nurse doing shift work. Her two Himalayan cats were left to their own devices in a tiny apartment high over the city. Although their behavior had not become too severe, their owner did not like what was going on. When the male became absolutely fed up with the loneliness and lack of stimulation, he jumped on the female and, according to the owner, quite viciously attacked her. He did not leave marks or draw blood; males very seldom hurt female cats.

The cat world works much better than ours. Some male cats do attack the females, not to hurt but only to warn or to break up a boring day. Attacking other males, of course, is quite a different story.

More quality playtime for the male with soft balls and toys soon straightened him out. Also, the owner will soon be retiring and will be able to spend more time with her cats. A happy ending.

As you can see, a pattern emerges in all these cases. All the cat mistakes are made over and over because the cat owners lack an understanding of their cats' nature. In the natural world, the cat had natural stresses: the excitement of the hunt, the sexual anxiety of mating, the concerns of motherhood, the interaction and territorial protection when encountering another cat. We in the modern world have taken away these stresses by taking the cat away from her natural habitat. But we have substituted some very unnatural stresses, stresses completely foreign to the cat's nature. Within the limits of what you have to work with, you can create a more satisfactory environment for your cat in her unnatural nineties habitat. Following my cat program and becoming more understanding of your cat's requirements will help you satisfy her basic needs and give her the good care she deserves.

QUESTIONS AND ANSWERS

Question

I bought a seven-week-old kitten from a pet store. She had always been in a cage and arrived at my house shy and frightened. She runs under the bed at any sound and is extremely nervous. What can I do to make her feel at home?

Answer

It will take a great deal of patience before this kitten is sure that she can trust you. Starting off her life in a cage at a pet store has been a major trauma for her. Let her go at her own pace and do not force your attentions on her. Play with her with soft balls and toys on the end of strings, and she will gradually learn to trust you.

She will probably always be a little scared of strangers and unexpected noises, but you will understand why and you will be gentle with her.

Question

I left my cat at a kennel for two weeks, and now that he is home he is a nervous wreck, chewing plants, meowing and full of anxiety. What is the matter with him?

Answer

The stress caused by his unfamiliar surroundings, perhaps

lack of kind care and the frightening barking of dogs were very upsetting for your cat. For now, give him as much extra attention as you can. The next time you go away, get someone to come into your house to look after your cat on his "home turf."

Question

My husband is jealous of our cat and says I give the cat more attention than I do him. I have had that cat much longer and I just cannot seem to help how I behave. What shall I do?

Answer

This is a common problem I see on my Kitty Calls. Although I know it is hard to change old habits, for your marriage's sake try to give your cat a little less attention — or your husband a lot more.

If you divide your attention equally and your husband is still jealous, perhaps he should look at his reasons for feeling jealous. None of this is your cat's fault, and your long-time pet shouldn't have to suffer.

Question

My cat is an indoor cat. Why does he chew my plants, and what can I do?

Answer

Three things come into play here: boredom, lack of greens in his diet and anxiety. It could be any or all three.

Try mixing a little chopped fresh lettuce into his food. Buy a box of cat grass, which is grown just for apartment cats to nibble on. Increase the amount of time you spend playing with your cat; maybe he is just bored with nothing to do.

Look at your lifestyle to see if your cat could be under any undue stress: too many "dont's" from his people; being hit, yelled at, teased by children or roughhoused; too much cigarette smoke that he has to breathe in, and so on.

Reorganize these areas and you will find your plants will be left alone.

Question

I have a very timid cat in a one-bedroom apartment and wonder if I should get another cat to keep him company.

Answer

In a small space with a cat who may not take to company, I would leave well enough alone. Cats need room, and cramped quarters can be stressful. Just enjoy the cat you have and do not ask for a problem.

Question

I am going on a long car trip with my ten-month-old cat. Should I give her a tranquilizer?

Answer

If your cat likes traveling by car, do not give her a tranquilizer. If she is absolutely terrified, though, and it is a trip you must make together, consult your vet. It is not a good idea to give your cat a pill of this kind unless absolutely necessary — and only as recommended by a vet.

Question

Can I take my two eighteen-year-old cats on a six-month trip to Europe?

Answer

Although I know how much you'd like to have your cats with you on a nice trip, it would be cruel to take two elderly cats on such an extended journey. The cats will be happier left at home with someone coming in to care for them.

Also, some countries apply stringent quarantine periods to pets. This would be unfair to your cats and would complicate your travel plans.

Question

My cat is terrified of going into her carrier. What can I do to make her more relaxed about it?

Answer

I assume this problem is longstanding. Keep the carrier open on the floor, not near your cat's food or litter. Put in a soft towel or cushion. Put in some catnip now and again, some tasty food treats and a new toy. In time she will go in of her own accord, and eventually she will forget her fear. The next time you have to carry her somewhere, she will not give you so much trouble.

Question

I have a cat, and I am thinking of moving in with a man who hates cats. What do you think about it?

Answer

Many of my housecalls are made where there is a great amount of friction over this very subject. In such households, the cat may become the scapegoat for any differences in the relationship, and he will suffer because of it.

Since you do not sound too sure about this move, perhaps you should give it more consideration before making this major change in your — and your cat's — lifestyle.

Question

Should I put a bird feeder where my cat can see it, since he is an indoor cat and I think it would amuse him?

Answer

Amuse, no. Torment, yes. Seeing so many birds will make your cat try to get outside and investigate.

Question

Can I go away for the weekend and leave my cat with enough food and water, or is this too long?

Answer

A weekend is definitely too long to leave a cat without having someone come in once a day to feed fresh food, change her litter, talk, stroke and play.

If your cat has a cat door and is used to going in and out, it is not so bad, but for an apartment cat or indoor cat this is too long to leave her alone. You can safely leave fresh food (never dry or semimoist), water and clean litter for one night and come back the next day to a grateful cat. Any longer than this and a friend or house-sitter should be called in.

....
THREE

Can You Pass the Cat Test?
Living with Your Cat

....

SO YOU WANT A CAT. Your friends have cats, you remember cats from your childhood and you think it is just what you need in your life. But *wait*. Do you know what the cat needs in *his* life? If you've read the first two chapters in this book, you will have a good idea by now of what makes a cat happy and healthy.

Is a cat really for you? Or, as the cat would put it, are you an ideal cat person? Could a cat fit into your lifestyle? Let's see how you measure up as a potential cat owner for the next twenty years. Does twenty years surprise you? Yes, a cat who is well looked after can live that long or longer, so you are taking on a long-term commitment with a little pet who will depend on you and you alone for his food, shelter, medical care, love, affection and companionship, and to make a lot of decisions that will affect his life. Does this sound like having children? The comparison isn't so farfetched. Having a pet is a big responsibility. This is a living creature you will be raising. If you think it's only a matter of opening a can of cat food once a day and cleaning the litter box once a week, *think again*. We're talking about a relationship, personalities, characters, companionship. So yes, I want you to stop, think and consider carefully so your pet will not become another statistic added to the list of millions of cats killed in North America and in Europe every year because of people's lack of understanding of the cat — and of themselves.

The following is a cat test that will make you think seriously about this major step in your life — acquiring a feline friend. Let me start with the hardest question:

WHY DO YOU WANT A CAT?

AS A COMPANION? As something to feel responsible for? As something to be dependent on you? As a decoration for your home? To be there for you even though you are never home? To replace a failed relationship? To keep you company through university? To give to your girlfriend for Christmas?

You can see your answers say a lot about whether the cat you acquire will in a short time end up at the animal shelter. If you think in terms of what you can do for the cat and not what it can do for you, and if you can honestly say you want your cat as a companion in a responsible relationship with a long-term commitment, you are ready for the next questions.

Can you afford it?

The first-time cat owner can find the cat is a rather expensive addition to the family, especially if diet and behavior are not first investigated and understood. A cat's poor health, mental or physical, can result in some steep vet bills. Costs for neutering or spaying, food, litter and shots can all mount up, and before you know it, the expense may be more than you can afford — and the cat is then added to that long list of disposables.

Before you decide to become a cat owner, sit down and calculate how much it will cost you in both money and time. Since your weekends and holidays must be organized around "who is going to look after the cat," you must add in the cost of the cat-sitter. (You cannot count on friends to come in and do this for you for the next twenty years.) Call your vet to find out the fees for neutering and spaying, the necessary shots and treating minor and major illnesses. Add the cost of litter, toys, scratching posts, brushes, elastic I.D. collar for the outdoor cat, and cat food (follow my suggestions in chapter 4 and save yourself a great deal of money).

Do you live in a house or an apartment? If a house, will you allow your cat to go outdoors? How large is your living space? A big house? A small bachelor apartment?

If you keep your cat indoors, he'll require more exercise and personal attention than an outdoor cat, who gets his fill of fun and excitement in his natural habitat. The smaller your living space, the more time you'll need to spend playing with your cat so he gets enough exercise, and you'll have to provide him with more toys to keep him occupied when you're not home. If you want to keep a cat in a small living space, better make sure you're a homebody. Boredom, behavioral problems and illness can set in quickly.

If you live in an apartment or condo, is there a "no pets" clause in your lease?

Do not take chances with this until changes are made to this cruel law. Do not put yourself in the painful position of having to choose between your cat and your home.

How many nights a week do you come home right after work and spend the whole evening at home? How many weekends in the year do you spend away from home? How often do you take lengthy vacations? How much time do you have in your day to play with your cat? Let your cat lie quietly on your lap? Do you feel silly talking to a cat?

All these questions relate to a central fact: your cat needs you. He relies on you to look after him and to give him the companionship he wants to give you in return. If you want a happy, healthy cat in a happy, healthy relationship, you have to give him quality time and you have to show him affection. You can't ignore your cat and expect him to entertain himself. I can't stress enough that you will have a relationship with your cat, and just as in a human relationship, it will not work out if you never do things together. If you're going to get a cat, you must be prepared to spend time playing with him, stroking him, brushing him, chatting with him, *being there* for him when he wants to come to you. If you spend most nights working or seeing friends, or if you're frequently away on business trips or you spend every weekend at your significant other's, maybe you shouldn't have a cat. He'll only be lonely and bored at home.

If you spend weekends at the cottage, will you take the cat with you?

Many cats don't enjoy traveling. All cats find a change in their environment stressful. If you are going to be away every weekend, your cat will be better off left at home with a pet-sitter. But if you *are* away every weekend, when are you going to find time for your lonesome cat?

Will you worry excessively if your outdoor cat doesn't come home one night?

It's understandable for a cat owner to be protective, but there are limits. Some people's need for their cat is so strong that they become anxious, oppressive owners, doing more harm than good. Cats need their freedom and their "space." Spayed females rarely wander far from home, but neutered males once in a while decide to go on a prowl. It is best to start some serious looking after one night's absence; someone may have turned your cat over to the Humane Society or an animal shelter for walking in their yard once too often. If you wait too long, your unclaimed cat may be put to sleep. In any event, your level of anxiety is a good measure of you as a cat owner. Cats get along best with relaxed, natural, reasonable owners; they don't enjoy frantic worrywarts.

How long will you likely be living where you are now? How many times have you moved to new quarters in the past five years? How long do your adult relationships last? That is, how many live-ins would your cat have to get used to in a year? Do you follow lots of routines at home, or are your days unscheduled?

Cats prefer stability, order and routine. Do these words describe your household? Or is it fast paced, hectic and disorderly? Cats are easily stressed by changes in their environment and the appearance on the scene of new people (and their pets). A stressed cat is not what you want to spend the next twenty years with.

Does the person you live with like cats, or would he or she just tolerate one for your sake?

Better not try. The first time something goes wrong, the person who "just tolerates" wants that cat out of the house, and you may have to choose between your partner and your cat. Don't take that chance, for the cat's sake.

Do you have a suitable cat household? How frequently do you have overnight houseguests? How often do your children have overnight guests? Do you play your stereo loudly? Do you play your TV loudly? How often do you or your children throw large, noisy parties at home? Do the adults in your house talk loudly? Do they argue maybe a little too often? Do the children in your house talk loudly? Do they argue maybe a little too often? Do you slam doors? Do you frequently use air-freshener sprays? Do you smoke? If your cat is an indoor cat, is there a room in your house — his "special room" — where he can go for peace and quiet and clean air?

Cats don't like strangers, loud noise or sudden noise, strong perfumy smells, cigarette smoke and so on. If these things characterize your household, please reconsider. If you have a generally quiet, stable home life, you should still make sure there's somewhere for that cat to retreat to — and I don't mean the basement or the hall closet — for the peace and solitude he so much prefers.

Do you have a new baby and now want to bring a new cat into your household?

This is not the time to get a cat. You are completely absorbed with your baby and won't be able to give your cat the time he needs. Wait until your child is at least seven before bringing a cat into your home. By that age, your child will be able to care for the cat responsibly and treat him with the kindness and gentleness he enjoys.

Do you have the time and patience to teach your children how to pick up and hold the cat, how to help feed and care for him? Would they learn to leave him alone if he so desired? Would they roughhouse with the cat?

It's crucial that your children learn about your cat's needs, just as you're taking the time to. Would they understand his need for peace and quiet and gentleness? Would they understand that teasing upsets him?

Are you prepared to make your unnatural habitat a suitable cat's home? If your cat will be an indoor cat, do you have wide window ledges or shelves by windows so he can sit there and look out? Will you buy or build him a "cat tree" and/or a large scratching post? Would you change a cat's water dish twice, if not three times, a day? How often would you clean your cat's litter box? If you were to have more than one cat, are you prepared to have one litter box per cat? Where would you put the litter boxes? In the bathroom? basement? hall cupboard? kitchen? near where your cat will eat or sleep?

These are questions of basic cat care, but it's frightening how many cat owners don't know or understand what's best for their pet. The smallest lapse can result in the most major behavioral problems. Read this book. If my program regarding feeding, litter boxes and exercise seems like too much trouble, maybe you should get goldfish instead and spare yourself and your cat a lot of grief.

Would you get your cat declawed?
No!

Would you get your cat spayed or neutered?

Yes!

How many other cats do you plan to own?

One cat is usually content if you're at home most evenings and on weekends. Two cats will keep each other company and play with each other while you're away at work. But make sure you have the space. Too many animals, or cramped quarters, can be stressful and can lead to behavioral problems.

If you found your cat scratching the furniture, would you shout at him and chase him away? Squirt him with a water gun? Hit him? Or would you gently take him to his own scratching post and encourage him to use it? If you found your cat up on the kitchen counter, would you throw something at him? Pick him up by the scruff of the neck and shake him? Or gently remove him and distract him by throwing a toy into the next room? If you came home and found a favorite ornament broken and your cat nowhere to be seen, would you hunt him down and spank him? Show him the broken object and yell at him? Or would you accept that with a cat in the house accidents sometimes happen and this is all part of being a cat owner? Would you understand that the love and companionship he gives you more than make up for a broken item now and again?

If you are not patient by nature, please don't get a cat. If you try to discipline your cat with force or violence, you'll only make him afraid of you. He'll run under the bed whenever you approach — and that's not the kind of pet you want. Patience and an understanding acceptance of the cat's nature are the keys to your healthy relationship.

Would you be prepared to make changes in your lifestyle to make your cat healthier and happier? Would you come home after work more often? Stay home for weekends more often?

Get up early on weekends to feed your cat? Go out to buy litter in a snowstorm? Change the litter box every day? Get up in the night to look after your sick cat?

I certainly hope so.

Is it Christmas, Easter, Valentine's Day or a birthday, and you want to surprise someone with a cat?

Don't. Giving someone a cat is not like giving someone a new sweater: a cat becomes a living, breathing part of your environment and a long-term responsibility. If the receiver is not ready for that responsibility, another cat will end up at the animal shelter, possibly destined to die.

Do you plan to give your mother, father or somebody else a cat because you think they need some company?

Don't. Maybe they have had enough responsibility in their lives and would only be stuck with a little creature they really did not want. I have seen this often. The person who will own the cat should be the only one to make the decision. Don't make it for them.

Now that you've thought seriously about getting a cat — and about yourself as a potential cat owner — just as you'd think seriously about, say, getting married or having children or moving to a new city or buying that new car, ask yourself once more: *Why do you want a cat?*

CHOOSING YOUR CAT

I F, AFTER ALL THIS SERIOUS thought, you are still ready for the responsibility and expense, let's get you a kitten. (Of course, if you do not feel like taking on an impish kitten, go for a fully grown cat, who will be most appreciative of his latter-day adoption and can be integrated into your home with a little less wear and tear on your nervous system.)

Although it's hard to resist, *do not* buy the first cat you see. Shop around, take your time. This is not a dress, a chair, a rug. This is a living, breathing creature, part of the natural stream of your life, a little cat-person who will be there for you when you are crying (purring, patting your face to give comfort), sharing new people and events in your life (cats are very curious and love to be part of new happenings in their own home). He will be a devoted companion, a friend who never talks back, only listens, and a hot-water bottle on your feet on a cold winter's night.

Where will you go for your new pet? The first place on your list should be the nearest Humane Society or animal shelter. Here you will see crowds of cats just waiting for a chance to escape from their cages into your loving home. (The problem will be choosing which one, because they all look so adorable and need homes so badly.) Here you will get a cat, for a modest fee, that has been checked by the shelter's vet, may already have been spayed or neutered and will probably come with some initial shots. What's more, you will know you have done a worthwhile thing in saving the life of this beautiful creature.

You should know that a cat from the shelter has had a hard time, but with your care and love he will definitely come around and make the best pet you have ever had. So if his coat is a little duller, if he is a little scared and timid, or perhaps a little aggressive, rest assured that when you get him home in your loving environment he will blossom into a perfect cat.

The other good way to get a kitten is from friends or neighbors whose cat has had kittens. Make sure you can go and see the kittens in their home, to be certain they are well looked after.

Two places you must beware of when getting your new cat: one is a "kitty mill" and the other is a pet shop.

Kitty mills are places where female cats are bred over and over — with no thought to the health of the mother or her kittens — solely for the purpose of making quick money. You can make sure you are not buying from a kitty mill by insisting on inspecting the home of your intended kitten. If on your search you find unhealthy surroundings for cats, report the mill to the nearest Humane Society or animal shelter, and it will be closed down. There are currently no regulations controlling who may breed cats, so a lot of cats are being sold from kitty mills.

Pet shops (which are supplied by kitty mills) are badly managed storehouses for domestic and exotic animals. The animals' welfare is not a concern; what counts here is how much the store can sell those caged creatures for, and how quickly. The conditions are often unclean, and the animals often poorly fed and poorly looked after. You may get lucky, but most people end up with big vet bills and more trouble than they bargained for when they fall in love with "that kitten in the window."

Until kitty mills are closed down and pet shops are forbidden to sell cats, you the cat buyer get no guarantee of anything with your purchase from these places.

"Let the buyer beware" applies also to cat breeders, who are unregulated and uninspected. If you are paying good money for a kitten from a breeder, make sure you can see where the cats are kept. Ask questions, and listen carefully to the answers. Does the breeder seem to have a good understanding of cats and cat care, or does it sound as if he or she just wants your money? A reputable breeder will have nothing to hide and should be a pleasure to deal with.

Whether you get your pet from an animal shelter or a friend, you should know how to recognize a healthy cat or kitten:

- the mouth and gums should be pink and the breath fresh
- the nose should be cool and moist, with no discharge
- the eyes should be bright, wide open, with no discharge

- the coat should be smooth and shiny, with no sores or bare patches
- the ears should be clean
- the breathing should be slow and quiet.

Although there are no guarantees at this young age, there are two cat behaviors that may influence your choice. One is that the kitten who runs out to greet you and demonstrates that he is not afraid of strangers will probably be outgoing and friendly during his life. The kitten who hangs back and seems to be the runt of the litter may well be quite shy during his lifetime. Depending on whether your household is quiet or noisy, you can, up to a point, tell which of these cats would better fit into your lifestyle. They will both make super pets, but, just like people, each cat has a different personality, depending on how he is treated in his first few weeks of life and how you treat him when you get him home.

All cats, whether quiet, outgoing, shy or playful, make wonderful pets. Each cat has his own definite personality shaped by his early surroundings, his owners and their lifestyle and how much of his natural needs are seen to. There is no guarantee that any kitten or cat will be 100 percent what you were expecting — but that is the beauty and fun of the cat.

There are about forty breeds of cats. Of course, a cat from any one of them would be a joy to own, but one in particular may have caught your fancy. Don't take him just because he looks nice. These are some of the questions you must ask the breeder or the shelter staff:

- Does this breed love to go outside, or would it be content indoors? (An indoor cat will need more exercise.)
- Is the cat very vocal? (A concern if you live in an apartment.)
- Does this breed like to be with children, or is it very

high-strung, preferring quieter adults?

- How often does this long-haired breed have to be groomed and what other physical care does it need?

(In my experience, a domestic short-hair, spayed or neutered, is more suitable as an apartment cat than most breeds. And with a daily combing, whether the cat is long-haired or short-haired, the hair ends up in the garbage and not all over your house.)

A reputable breeder or the staff at an animal shelter will be glad to answer all your questions and would not want the cat to end up in a home that would not be good for him. Remember, this is a twenty-year commitment, and care at this stage means a mistake will not be made that will mean heartbreak for your family and pain to the cat.

Now, off you go, armed with this practical information, confident that you know a healthy kitten (or cat) when you see one, that you are aware of dishonest cat people and that you are not going to buy the first cat you see. He will be yours for years to come, and you want a good fit into your lifestyle.

SETTING UP YOUR HOME FOR YOUR CAT

TRY TO GET YOUR NEW FAMILY member when you have some holidays so you can spend at least the first few days making him feel at home and letting him get to know you. He will want to sleep with you at night, will want four or five little meals every day (see "Food" in chapter 4) and will want to just have you there so when he gets a little frightened by his new surroundings — and he will — he can run to your lap for comfort. *Don't* dump him in the door and go to work or away for the weekend.

The first thing you must do before bringing your cat home is buy the best cat carrier you can afford. Whether you travel by foot, car or bus, your cat should always be securely contained — one leap and he can be gone in a strange neighborhood, and a cat loose in the car can get underfoot and cause a serious accident.

The second thing you must do before bringing your cat home is set up his own "special room." (See the section "Moving Blues — The Value of the Special Room" in chapter 2.) Especially if he's a kitten, you might consider using your bedroom as the special room. In this room have a bowl of water, a small amount of food and a clean litter box. For a kitten, set up a cozy carton with a blanket inside, and raised off the ground to avoid drafts.

When you get home with your cat, take him, still in his carrier, straight to his room and open the carrier door. Let him come out and inspect the room at his leisure. Do not interfere with his inspection. Keep your cat in this room for a couple of days or until he seems to feel relaxed in his new surroundings. Gradually let him out to investigate the rest of your house. Let him go at his own pace. It probably won't be long before he's right at home everywhere and finding little nooks and crannies to hide in.

A kitten should be neutered or spayed before he starts on his outdoor journeys. And a new cat should be kept indoors for a few weeks, to establish a sense of home, before being let outside. His first trips should be supervised; he'll probably be glad to know you're nearby to help out if there's trouble.

There — that's all there is to it. The cat magic has begun!

FOUR

Your Cat's Well-Being:
How to Care for Your Cat
···

CATS IN THE NINETIES LOVE PEOPLE who understand their nature and provide them with a good cat life, so I cannot emphasize too strongly my "Five-Point Strategy for Well-Adjusted Cats":

1. Provide fresh food.
2. Change litter every day.
3. Exercise — inside and out.
4. Spay and neuter.
5. *Never* declaw.

By following these important cat care rules, you will avoid behavioral problems and guarantee your cat a long and healthy life, one that's as natural as it can be in the modern urban jungle.

FOOD

YOU ARE WHAT YOU EAT. How often have you heard this expression? Too often, I am sure, but it is true. I realize how very important what I eat is to my moods, my energy and my weight. Yet in this age of McDonald's, frozen foods, microwaves, "lite" foods, overeating, undereating and masses of vitamins and diet pills, the people of the nineties are consuming a grand mess of strange things and doing it at an extremely fast pace.

The motto of today is "If it's quick it has to be good." Good-tasting? Maybe. But good for us? Never. The long list of chemicals that appears on tinned, frozen and packaged foods is a great worry to people of the nineties, who are turning to a fresh and natural approach to what they eat. It is a fact that children are physically and emotionally affected by the additives in their food, and it is my belief that some of the cat's problems are directly related to the buildup of these many chemicals in their small and fragile bodies. I feel the best thing we can do for the cat of the nineties is feed her the freshest food possible.

As I go about on my Kitty Calls, I am constantly shocked at what people think their dear old puss can live on. A dish of dry food, a bowl of water, and off they go. Is this a penthouse or a jail? It does not matter if the owners are rich or poor, because everyone is in a big hurry. In response, manufacturers have come up with these wonderful marketing items called "dry" and "semimoist" food, and that's what thousands of cats are getting as their *only* food.

We don't have to be taught that fresh fruits, vegetables, grains, fish and meat prepared in a variety of ways make us healthy, just as our cat knows what's best for her — and it is *not* dry food and water.

At London Zoo, in England, one of the major concerns is how best to feed animals in their unnatural habitats (which our cats are in, in our apartments and houses). Every day truckloads of fresh fruits, vegetables, meats, fish and dairy products are brought in for the zoo animals, in many varieties to suit each species' needs and tastes. Nothing but the freshest will do, since the expert animal keepers know how crucial fresh food is to the health of animals in captivity. The keepers do not spend all day dishing out canned food (or as I call it, "plastic food"). They know that smell, texture and variety are what keep up the animals' interest and joy in life.

The same applies to "house cats in captivity." A cat who is kept indoors all her life needs all the help she can get, and food is the most important part of her daily life. If all she has to look forward to every day is dry food and water, depression will quickly set in, and we all know that depression leads to illness and behavioral problems.

When I opened the Cats' Cradle, my bed and breakfast for cats, some ten years ago, it was an innovation, and I made my own rules, always keeping the comfort and health of the cats my first priority. I decided I would have each client tell me what their cats liked to eat and I would do my very best to feed them as they were fed at home. At least then, in the strange environment of my home, they would have the food they were used to. I assumed I would have to have on hand liver, chicken, sardines, my own mixture of ground beef and veggies, chicken livers and a host of other healthy, natural foods.

Much to my surprise, people arrived with boxes of dry food, packages of semimoist food, various assortments of tins and, more often than not, cases of expensive foods that could be purchased only from their vet and that their cat *had* to eat.

This was all new to me. I had always lived in a simple, natural, common-sense way, and there was never a lot of money for tins and fancy packages, especially when I knew that fresh was the healthy way to go. Be that as it may, I wanted my clients (cats and people) to be happy, so on each cat's file card I duly noted its tastes and each cat was fed its tin, dry or semimoist as requested.

At that time I was much too busy with my hundreds and hundreds of feline guests to do more than wonder if all those foods were really good for the animals. But today, as I deal with the psychological problems of cats, I must investigate each aspect of their lives to uncover what is causing the disturbance. And I find food plays a major part in these behavioral problems.

Probably the most complete food for cats would be ground-up mice, but obviously this would not make good advertising fodder. Today's fast-paced cat owners have no time to wonder just what is in all the expensive, glitzily packaged cat food. They just buy and hope that the so-called experts are not misleading them. Well, with the multibillion-dollar (and growing) pet food industry more than well established in North America, Britain and Europe, questions about the quality and contents of all this pretty packaging are long overdue.

For those of you wondering if you must buy all this expensive cat food to do right by your cat — no, you do not. Your cat will be better off if you take her diet in hand yourself. As a human concerned for your well-being, you may already be choosing fresh, natural foods over chemically laden, expensively packaged foods. And if you're concerned for your cat's well-being, you'll do her the same favor.

(My recommendations for a good cat diet are suitable both for those of you who can afford to pamper your cat and those of you living on a more modest budget. Those of you who cook every day, you are the big money savers where your cat is concerned, and your cat will be the healthiest.)

My cousin's cat recently died after twenty wonderful years in his natural habitat — outdoors, in a small town. I asked my cousin what she had fed him. She said he ate raw liver and cream, with all the treats he could get on the side. Now, I do not like a cat to get raw anything (cooking kills bacteria and worms, which is the same reason we cook most of what we eat), but this just goes to show you what a cat's basic need is: meat. And although "milk" seems to be a dirty word these days when mentioned in the same breath as "cat," I still believe cats and milk go together. Granted, some breeds cannot tolerate milk, but for the domestic cat, fresh milk, *not* ice-cold from the fridge but slightly warmed, is a nutritious food. Fresh water should be left down at all times. You may catch your cat drinking out of the sink or the tub, but *never* let her drink out of the toilet. Even if it looks clean, it might contain germs, and residues of chemical cleaners can poison your cat.

Since protein is the cat's first dietary requirement, when you are cooking meat for yourself or your family, before the spices and sauces go on, put a little plain cooked meat aside for your cat (*no bones*, to be on the safe side.) Add some vegetables and a small amount of starch — potatoes or pasta — and you have a wonderful meal for a cat. As well as cow's liver, chicken livers, beef, veal, pork and poultry, any kind of fish you are having can be prepared in the same way. Don't forget to mash the fish well to make the bones safe for eating. Also offer cheeses. Twice a week, give her cooked eggs, alone or mixed with her favorite foods. Include milk, plain or diluted, once a day, a little butter twice a week to keep her coat shiny, and half a tin of sardines (in water or oil — the oil is good for her coat), salmon, tuna or other seafood once in a while.

Experiment to see which veggies your cat likes and whether she prefers them mixed up or separate in her dish. Cats can be fussy about vegetables. If yours doesn't seem to like any, chop up some lettuce and mix it into her food once or twice a week. (Outdoor cats eat all the grass they want, but you may wish to grow, or buy pots of ready-grown, cat grass — sometimes called cat barley — as a treat. Put the whole pot — dirt and all — down on the floor and watch your cat feast happily.)

Feed your cat like this twice a day, morning and evening. No between-meal snacks, please. Indoor cats who nibble all day quickly become fat and unhealthy.

For those rushed times, or if you're not cooking or you're cooking something your cat won't eat, keep on hand a supply of baby foods in reusable jars. You can serve junior meats to mature cats and pureed meats to kittens. (For more on feeding kittens, see "The Very Young and the Very Old Cat" later in this chapter.)

Those of you who don't eat breakfast (shame!) may be wondering what to feed your cat in the mornings. Pop a little frozen meat or fish or some baby food into the microwave.

That and some warm milk make an excellent start to your cat's day.

This high-protein, sensible, fresh diet will keep your cat perky and looking forward to new smells and textures at each meal. Her teeth will be strong, her coat glossy, and she'll be full of life. And since the portions are not large for a cat and you're buying the food for yourself anyway, you will find this a much more economical and practical way of feeding your cat. You will never have to worry about running out of cat food, or making the difficult choice of which brand to buy, or becoming anxious over the fact that advertising says this food and that prevents all sorts of feline diseases (it simply is not true).

Another benefit of this program is that because your cat gets the variety she desires, if she is sick and goes off one food, she can eat something else. When cats who eat the same thing every day (even food prescribed by the vet) are sick and stop eating, very often they're in no mood to start eating something they're not accustomed to — and not eating doesn't help your cat get better.

A final point. *Never* feed your cat dry or semimoist food. These are too often linked to painful (and sometimes fatal) urinary tract disorders. Don't risk it! If you know you're going to get home late at night, don't put down dry nibbles for your cat. She isn't going to starve; she'd rather wait for you to serve her a delicious, healthy meal.

Now for those of you with lots of money and no time, you who eat out most nights of the week, order in on weekends and grab a fast lunch, I cannot change *your* bad habits, but I beg, for your cat's sake, that you do the following:

Give your cat baby-food meats. These are cheap, come in a variety of flavors and contain no chemicals. But provide your cat with a healthy support diet, too. Once a week buy chicken livers, or beef or calf liver, and simmer in a little water until cooked. Let cool, then give your cat one meal and freeze the rest in individual meal-size packages. Two or three times a week, when flying by the kitchen, defrost a serving. You can also cook up and freeze chicken, fish and so on, though the liver is very important for your cat. Also, when you are making an omelette or scrambling eggs on the weekend, throw in an extra egg for your cat — she will love it. A half tin of mashed sardines, salmon, shrimps, crab or lobster once or twice a week is a lot better for your cat than cat food. Milk, cheese and a little butter rounds out the diet. In between these high-protein meals, serve baby foods.

This program is second best, but in this age of fast we cannot always be perfect. Still, even you must cook something at some time, so when the memorable event takes place, remember your pet and share it with her.

The food on your table tonight is not the "table scraps" that corporate pet food people would like you to believe. It is the purest, freshest food you can feed your cat — since it is what you yourself are eating — and it does not get any better than that. If you truly care for your cat, take her diet in hand, tie it in with your budget and feed her naturally, with a minimum of chemicals.

Start right now — cook up a batch of chicken livers. It will do you both good!

LITTER

C AT LITTER IS A BILLION-DOLLAR business in North America, but as I make my Kitty Calls I find that too many people are not using it properly, which in the cat's new habitat (indoors) results in serious behavioral problems that cause misery for the cat owner, anxiety for the cat and, in thousands of instances, death for those cats who fail to use their litter boxes at all.

Understanding the nature of the cat in her natural habitat will be a big help to the cat owner. When a cat decides to "use the bathroom" in her natural habitat (outside), she first looks around to see if anyone is watching. The cat has a natural desire for privacy and always looks for a private spot. (She wants to avoid predators while she's occupied.) If she feels extremely safe on her territory, she will sometimes not worry so much about privacy, but generally she will pick a quiet corner of the garden, dig a small hole, relieve herself and carefully cover up her natural fertilizer. She never uses the same spot twice. A 50-by-150-foot litter box is hers and she likes it just that way.

The cat's nose is extremely sensitive to all smells, and a litter box that has sat in a small cupboard or in a basement for a whole week, with maybe only the feces removed, is a nightmare for the clean cat. What is she to do? Go against everything nature is saying to her and use the box? Or wet the bed, which is oh so clean? Nature being what it is, there is no choice here — clean gets it every time.

The reaction from her irate owners is disturbing and traumatic for the cat, who understands none of it. Remember, although this is your baby, your confidante, your companion and your captive friend, this is not a person. This is a *cat*, and she can act only in a catlike manner — and that means she has to have *clean*. So, to get you off on the right foot, I will tell you the proper way to 100-percent success with your cat and her litter box.

First of all, buy the largest plastic litter box you can find, and buy one for each cat. I do not recommend the ones with the hoods, which uncomfortably confine a cat's movements. If you put the box in a quiet spot, your cat will have all the privacy she needs. A quiet basement corner is a good place, or a spare room or attic room (but beware of "out of sight, out of mind"). In an apartment, a storage room or den is okay. The bathroom is all right only if you live alone; otherwise it probably gets too much traffic. Avoid busy places such as stairways, landings or open areas. Wherever you place the box, make sure your cat has enough room to maneuver and that she isn't hemmed in by walls, coats or the toilet. Apply Cat Rule #3, Do unto others . . . Ask yourself if *you* had to use the litter box, where would you want it?

Line each pan with a plastic liner from your pet supply store or supermarket and put in a reasonable amount of litter, about two inches — not too much, because you are going to *change the litter every day*, yes, *every day*. This is the secret to your cat's happiness when it comes to the litter box. In the rush of the nineties, people too often make the mistake of scooping out only the feces and changing the box only once or twice a week. If you leave the urine sitting there all the time, you're asking for trouble. You may grow accustomed to the odor and not notice it, but your visitors will. And so will your cat, who will prefer to go elsewhere. So, every day just fold up the sides of the plastic liner, tie them together and lift out the dirty litter. Slip in a new liner and pour in new litter. It's all over in less than a minute. Your cat will always have a clean, fresh-smelling box to use, and you will always have a clean, fresh-smelling house.

Now if you have more than one cat in a small apartment, there may not be space for a litter box for each cat. One will have to do. *But* you will have to clean it out — of wet and dry — in the morning and completely change it in the evening (or vice versa).

Your cat may be overzealous when it comes to scratching in the litter box, and she may tear the liners. (You may also find them too expensive.) In that case, by all means use the unlined litter box, but be sure you give it a complete soapy scrubbing once a week. If you do use liners, a good wash once a month should be sufficient. Use mild detergents — dish soap or even shampoo — rather than strong chemical cleansers or bleach, which may harm your cat. Replace your litter boxes once a year. Because they are plastic, they absorb odors and stains.

If you are one of those poor souls who for months or even years has been plagued with a cat who has been turning your house into a large litter box, I have the solution for you.

First, understand *why* your cat isn't using her litter box. Begin by taking her to the vet for a checkup. A litter problem is sometimes a physical problem.

I see many causes of a litter problem. Among the most common:

- It could be just a case of a dirty litter box, and so the problem is easily cleared up immediately.

- A succession of traumas (see chapter 2) eventually leads the cat into a state of anxiety. Just like an anxious child, she becomes a bedwetter.

- Poor diet (especially one of dry food only) and lack of exercise leads to the cat population — males especially — being plagued with urinary problems such as feline urinary syndrome. After suffering the pain of a urinary infection, the cat never forgets where he experienced that pain — and most of the time it was in his litter box, which he subsequently wants to avoid. Just as in humans with bladder or kidney infections, urinating or straining to urinate is painful. As well, he may experience feelings of having to urinate, but nothing will come out, or of not feeling he has to urinate and then having an accident. All this leads the fastidious cat into deep confusion, so that after a bout of urinary complaint, unless he is guided kindly and carefully through his illness, the litter problem becomes a great problem indeed. (And we come back again to preventive cat care: good food, exercise, no traumas and more understanding of your cat's nature.)

To cure your cat of her litter problem, first you must turn a space into what I call the "special room." (See the section "Moving Blues — The Value of the Special Room" in chapter 2.) Think of your cat as being temporarily emotionally disturbed and needing a long rest, because that is just what is happening. The room should be well ventilated and have no rugs or broadloom on the floor. (If the only room you can use does have broadloom, set up a cat tree beside a window, left open an inch or so for fresh air. Hang toys from the cat tree and put your cat's favorite bedding on one of the platforms. You want to encourage her to get off the floor so she will forget her bad habit.) Put down a large, clean litter box and *change it every day.* Your cat's food and water bowls go on the other side of the room, away from the litter box, and her favorite toys, her scratching post and her favorite bedding should all be provided. Shut your cat into her room whenever you go to work or out shopping, knowing that when you come home you will not find any unpleasant surprises. If the room contains a bed, the mattress should be removed or covered with a large sheet of aluminum foil (tape sheets together to form a cover for the bed). Cats hate to walk on aluminum foil. This also goes for furniture you can't remove. Never cover anything with sheets of plastic; there is something about plastic that makes some cats urinate on it. Cats will urinate on soft items — bathmats, duvets, pillows, cushions, towels — so the room should be stripped bare. You do not want your cat to be tempted at the very beginning of her treatment.

Do not think of this as a punishment for your cat. When a cat has a litter problem, there is only one thing you can do — cure it. You must be firm. I have had clients say to me, "But she won't be happy shut in a room," or "I could never do that — I would be so unhappy," or "He will think I don't love him anymore." As a cat owner, you are always in charge, and you must make the decisions for your cat. She depends on you, and she cannot stop a litter problem by herself. *You must do it for her.*

Since I would never do anything cruel to a cat, and since I have had so much success with my litter program, I ask you to be patient and firm. The door is shut, making your cat feel safe; in most cases, other things in the house are causing or adding to her anxiety, and they are not going to bother her in that room. If your cat is an outdoor cat, she can be either outside or in her special room. If she is an indoor cat only, this room will be her home until you have your house cleaned up and she is using her litter box properly. If your cat hates it in there and cries and scratches to get out, you will have to bear it, knowing that there is no alternative and that this program is best for your cat. The more you put into the program, the sooner it will be a success. Be firm.

Now, while you know where your cat is and, most important, what she is doing, you can get on with the job of putting your house back in shape.

There are two steps to reclaiming your house.

One is eliminating the cat's scent in all the areas she has used. Otherwise, when she comes out of her special room, she may wet where her scent remains, starting the whole vicious cycle all over again. All badly soiled broadloom will have to be taken up and the floor underneath thoroughly cleaned with strong soapy water, then rinsed with a half-and-half mixture of vinegar and water. All walls, windowsills, cushions and so on will have to be washed, and curtains and drapes dry-cleaned. Absolutely everything that has been sprayed or soiled must be thoroughly cleaned to remove the scent.

The next step is to make those areas where your cat is used to spraying or soiling very distasteful, in natural ways, so that she will never use those places again. Spray the areas with cologne or perfume, especially one with a citrus scent. Cats do not like perfume of any kind and will stay right away from the treated area. Just to be on the safe side, put fresh lemon, lime or orange peels over the area (remember, this is only temporary until you have your cat turned around). When she comes out of her special room for her first walk, all she will get from the rest of the house will be fresh, clean (and to her hated) smells on what were once her favorite litter areas. As a final safeguard, cover the once soiled areas, if possible, with sheets of aluminum foil. You have now turned all soiled areas into minefields for your cat, but have done so in a natural way.

When you are ready, since *you* are now in charge of your home, let your cat out of her room for short, supervised periods, increasing in length every day. Believe me, when she has a choice between that beautiful clean litter box in her special room, which you clean every day, and all those foul odors coming from her once favorite spots, your troubles are over. As long as there are no accidents, you can leave her out, but never, in the beginning, leave her unsupervised for a long time. Before you leave for work or go out in the evening or go to bed, remember to put your cat in her room.

The amount of time for the special room program depends on each household, how much work you put into it and how strictly you follow the program. In a few weeks you should see a great improvement, and eventually your cat will be on the right path, permanently. The horrible specter of having to put your beloved pet to sleep is no longer with you every day. Your home is fresh-smelling and clean, and your feelings of helplessness at not knowing what to do are over. The quality of your cat's life is now enriched. And if ever by chance you have a little accident, you now have the tools to work with and need not panic. Common sense, natural methods and an understanding of your cat's nature are all the equipment you need to solve this distressing problem.

This program has worked for hundreds of my clients, and it will work for you.

PLAY AND EXERCISE

JOGGING, AEROBICS, WALKING, cycling, swimming — the list goes on and on of the ways we humans choose to keep ourselves in shape. But what about your cat?

If she goes outside, exercise is not your concern (though of course you will want to play with her when you are both in the mood). She is up and down trees, stalking and chasing everything that moves, from leaves to bugs to other cats, and generally keeping a watchful eye on her territory.

But what about the one-room cat, the apartment cat or even the house cat who can't go outside — how does she get her exercise? What can you do to keep her perky and happy in a narrow cat environment?

Well, you can plan to come home more often, for a start. And once you're at home, there are many simple and afford-able things you can do within the cat's nineties environment that will help relieve her tension, stimulate her and make her happy.

You will already (I hope) have purchased the largest scratching post or cat tree you can find, or have made one yourself, or have brought in a real tree trunk or piece of driftwood. This gives your cat a center for her exercise, play and grooming activities. Here she sharpens her claws, stretches, enjoys familiar smells on the area, plays with all her favorite toys nearby — she warms up in this area, getting ready for action. If you watch for your cat's signal, you will know when it's time for you to join in the fun.

Two games cats love are hide-and-seek and chase-and-sometimes-retrieve-the-ball. Playing these simple games once a day will exercise your cat in her confined space; this will keep her weight down, relax her body and promote good muscle tone and circulation, which in turn will help keep your vet bills down and add healthy years to your cat's life.

When your cat shows signs of wanting action, especially in the evening (you will not want your sleep disturbed by a restless cat), go into another room, stand behind the door and call your cat's name in her favorite way. When she comes, pop out quietly (don't scare her) and say boo. Then run (again, not so you scare her) to another room and again call and wait. Your cat will gradually learn the game and look forward to it. As she follows you from room to room, she gets the exercise she needs *and* gets to play in a cat way —

not being picked up, roughhoused or teased, but played with in a fun, gentle, harmless way.

For the ball game, buy at a pet supply store some small soft balls, the kind cats can get their teeth into. If your cat loves to retrieve, as lots of cats do, throw the ball and let her go for it. If she brings it back, fine. Just keep tossing it and your cat will get her nightly exercise.

If your cat does not bring back the ball, don't worry. Every cat is different, just as we all are. Retrieve the ball yourself and throw it again. Your cat will get her much needed exercise chasing the ball here and there.

Some cats think it's great fun if you get down on the floor with them and try to steal back the ball. Give it a few wiggles — as if it's a struggling mouse — and let your cat work hard to keep it.

If you have children in the house from two years and up, teach them to play with the cat the same way. Little ones tend to want to lug the cat around, which she hates, or tease the cat, which she also hates. Constructive playtime makes everyone happy.

Another good game for the cat and young children — and grownups — is to pull a string around with a little cat toy tied on the end and let your cat chase it. You can go up and down stairs, around corners, over the furniture, and as fast as you can.

Toys don't have to be expensive, and with a little imagination you can make many of them at home. Cats love old socks (roll one up with some catnip and stuff it into the other, then knot it securely), rolled-up nylons, paper bags, cardboard boxes, cardboard bathroom tissue rolls, onion bags with a ball or catnip mouse inside, bows from birthday presents, wine corks, a tightly wound ball of wool . . . the possibilities are endless. And of course they'll find their own — pencils, lipstick, you name it. (As with medicines and children, if you don't want your cat to get it, put it out of reach.) Avoid toys that have eyes, ears, bells, buttons or strings that can be chewed off and swallowed. And of course avoid plastic bags.

A couple of important points. Be sure to stop when your cat has had enough. If she starts to pant or her mouth hangs open or she simply loses interest, stop at once. Some exercise is good, but a cat does not need *too* much to be happy. And of course you would not encourage a cat to exert herself in hot weather.

Also remember that a cat loves a good time, but a *cat* good time. Play with your cat in a way the cat likes, not the way you the human like. And never be rough, sudden, loud or otherwise frightening. But if she flicks her tail, growls, puts her ears back or bares her claws, she's saying, "I've had enough. Please back off."

Spay and Neuter

HAVE YOU EVER SEEN a female cat when she comes into her first heat, so thrilled with her sexuality? Have you ever seen the tomcats pounding up the sidewalk on determined feet to find this beautiful lady? Have you ever seen the most devoted mother in the world nursing her first batch of perfect kittens?

No, probably not. Not everyone is so privileged. But I have, and it only goes to prove that nature is wonderful. Unfortunately this natural picture becomes the big-city reality: What are we going to do with all these kittens?

While you are enjoying the fun of them, though maybe starting to worry because no one seems to want a kitten, the nursing mother's body is already set to make the next batch of kittens. If nature takes its course, in less than a year you may have ten kittens to find homes for. Straight to the vet you go with the mother, and rightly so. She *must* be spayed. This is not the era for "whole" cats.

Or you have recently become the proud owner of a beautiful male cat. You are not sure about the neutering procedure, so you've decided to wait and see what happens.

The very handsome fellow has now taken to staying out all night and coming home with deep, infected sores, the result of machismo in the cat world. He sleeps all day and does not respond to your efforts to play and pet. He is sometimes dirty and smelly and not something you want to find sleeping on your bed. Even worse, he begins to spray to mark his territory inside your house. This is the lifestyle of a "whole" or unneutered tom; that is how nature has made him to be. But we have brought him into our home and we do not like him this way.

What to do? Well, in this day and age there is nothing else to do. He *must* be neutered. Not only for your sake, but for the sake of all those unwanted and uncared-for kittens he is fathering. I repeat, this is not the era for "whole" cats.

Although I believe 100 percent in spaying and neutering, I cannot stress enough that this is the *only* trauma (and it is a trauma, make no mistake) that we should put our cats through in order that they may better fit into our nineties urban lifestyle.

Your spayed female will be spared the wearying, weakening cycle of bearing litter after litter. You'll be spared hearing her howl and having her more interested in mating than in you when she's in heat. Your neutered male will become much less aggressive; he'll be gentler and much more content with home and hearth. He'll stop spraying. If he's an outdoor cat, he'll stop fighting, cutting down considerably on your vet bills. Both sexes will be calmer and more loving.

DECLAWING

> Question: I read somewhere that cat owners sometimes have their cats "declawed." Is this operation advisable if the animal is destructive?

> Answer: Veterinary removal of the claws (onychectomy) is a painful mutilation which cannot be recom-

mended under any circumstances. Cats with their nails removed are deprived of an important defence mechanism and have difficulty in climbing. Many continue to behave as if they were still able to sharpen their claws, and some undergo a profound personality change following surgery. The operation is very seldom performed in Great Britain, though more often, I am sorry to say, in North America. Any cat which has been declawed is automatically disqualified from cat shows under the rules which are in force in most countries. The operation is often performed at three or four months old but if not properly performed one or more claws can grow back. If the only way you can tolerate a cat is after this dreadful mutilation, then you should not keep one at all.

The above was taken from *The Cat Care Question and Answer Book* by the British vet Dr. Barry Bush, BVSc, Ph.D, FRCVS.

For anywhere from $150 to $250 (far more than the cost of a good scratching post) a cat can be taken to almost any vet in North America, have her claws and claw beds removed, spend three days in a cage wondering what in the world she did to deserve this, then be taken home and expected to be her cute little self. Is this any way to treat our loving friend?

If I took you to a doctor and he pulled out your fingernails and toenails (and the beds! — I shudder to think what that entails), left you in agony in a small cage, frightened, surrounded by strangers, for three days, how would you feel about life and people?

What has happened to us here in North America that we so casually and routinely perform this surgery? Have we become so cruel and callous that we will go to any lengths to protect our material goods — the furniture? Or do we let so-called professionals guide us in everything we do without our stopping to think. Yes, that is the operative word. *Think* for yourself.

We have a moral obligation to creatures who depend on us for safekeeping and well-being. We must learn to do the right thing without the dollar coming into play. Unfortunately here in North America fast solutions to problems lead to long-term misery.

A cat who has been declawed cannot climb properly, either for exercise or to escape danger. She cannot scratch, and so cannot exercise all her muscles. She is unable to grip some of her toys. She is unable to defend herself. After the operation it doesn't take her long to figure out these changes. Feeling vulnerable and defenseless, she lives in a constant state of fear and anxiety. Withdrawal and hiding are the least severe of many resulting behavioral problems.

Please, stop this obscenity now.

For you who have already had your cat declawed, I say "what's done is done." In the nineties we naturally look to experts for advice, and if you were badly advised, it cannot be helped. But now that you know how cruel declawing is, you will not have it done again.

For those of you who have about $200 to spend on declawing, my advice is to rush to your nearest pet supply store and buy the biggest scratching post or cat tree (or both) available. Keep in mind that it must sit on the floor or against the wall, without moving. If it moves even a fraction, take a large nail and anchor it solidly to the floor or wall, or fasten it to a wide wooden base.

If you are handy with tools or can obtain a sturdy log, you can save the whole $200 by making your own scratching post. Remember, you are replacing your cat's natural habitat. Think "tree" and you can't go wrong. Anchored, solid and large. You will then have $50 to $100 to donate to your local animal shelter. The physical pain and mental anguish you spare your cat cannot be measured in dollars.

You also guarantee yourself a cat who has suffered one less major trauma, making her physically and mentally healthy and cutting down on your future vet bills.

If you have a cat who scratches in the wrong place — the furniture, usually — get your new scratching post ready and work with your common sense and knowledge of the cat to discourage her from scratching where you don't want her to. Here is how.

Keeping in mind that the natural way is the best way, every day affix fresh lemon, lime or orange peels to the scratched spot. (Be safe. Don't use pins, which your cat might swallow.) You can also dab on Tabasco sauce if the fabric is dark and will not show the stain. Also, a heavy perfume or cologne sprayed on the area will keep your cat away. She detests all these smells. When your cat ambles over for a good scratch on the arm of the couch, she gets a whiff of hated smells and quickly moves on. But where to? To her new scratching post, of course. (You might have to carry her there a few times, until she associates the need with the proper place.)

Rub her scratching post with a little catnip to make it more attractive. As well, turn the scratching post into a fun cat area. Dangle toy mice on strings from it and let your cat leap up to play with them. During this play, she will automatically scratch on the post. If you play with her regularly, she will soon learn to love her new play area. Your sofa or chair, smelling strongly of citrus and perfume, will be no fun at all. And you will no longer have to worry about your furniture, because you will have given the cat back a most important part of her habitat — the tree.

CATS AND CHILDREN

I 'VE HEARD IT SUGGESTED that boys who have pet cats to love grow up to be a little less than men. What utter rubbish! A case in point is Ernest Hemingway, America's number-one author and adventurer, who was considered a real man's man. He owned forty cats — all at once! — and had this to say of them: "A cat has absolute emotional honesty: human beings, for one reason or another, may hide their feelings but a cat does not." Animals have a way of making children — girls *and* boys — feel relaxed and happy and less lonely.

By all means get your little boy a cat, and never for one moment think his love of cats will make him a sissy. Children who learn compassion for animals, any animal, are likely to find it in their hearts to show compassion for their fellow human beings. Children (boys *and* girls) should learn at a very early age kindness and gentleness and to look after things more dependent than themselves so that when they grow up they will take good care of their own families, friends and the less fortunate in society. All this they learn by properly raising their own cats, with care and understanding.

Children under the age of seven do not need a pet. There is a time when very small children are naturally not responsible for simple cat care and not ready to follow "leave the cat alone" rules. Although cats seem to understand that small children have little control and are usually tolerant of their behavior, they are quite frightened when they cannot get away from the young child. The cat is generally not happy in such a household, which is why most animal shelters will not adopt a cat out to a home where there are very young children. As well, if you give a cat to a very young child, the child may soon get bored with the novelty and move on to other things, neglecting the cat.

If you already have a cat plus small children or toddlers, please try to let the cat get away for most of the day. Let her out if she's an outdoor cat; if she is an indoor cat, establish a nice quiet nest for her and put her there as often as possible.

Between seven and ten years is a good age for a child to get a cat; he or she is now ready to learn how to behave with an animal. Children should first be taught to pet the cat gently. No roughhousing — ever. They should also be shown the proper way to pick up the cat. A cat should be picked up by putting one hand under her chest behind her front legs and the other under her rear end, supporting her weight, and then slowly lifted. *Never* pick her up by her tail, by the scruff of her neck or only under the front body, leaving her hanging uncomfortably. Teach your child not to *make* your cat do anything, as this is a sure way to annoy her. Last, the child should learn not to put his or her face into the cat's, but to reach out a gentle hand. The cat may be hot, irritated or just not in the mood, and may lash out.

There is no reason that an older child should not have the job of feeding the cat and making sure she has clean water every day. It is maturing for children to know they are responsible for their little pet — it gives them a feeling of self-worth and accomplishment, important elements in the growth of self-esteem. An older child might be taught to change the litter box every day and/or let the cat in and out when needed. In these days of enormous stress on parents, assigning such jobs cuts down on your work and builds your child's character.

What with today's psychological stress and there not being enough time for anything, it is so important not to overextend yourself with commitments. If you have a full-time job, a house to run and a new baby, taking on a cat in addition would not be a wise move. The pleasant picture of home and hearth filled with children and animals is one of yesteryear. If you try to live this fantasy when you don't have the time, the cat is the one to suffer, through neglect and perhaps being given up to the animal shelter when the family discovers her to be more work than they can manage. So if your life is now full with baby, job and home, please, for the cat's sake, do not bring in a cat.

If your cat is already an established member of your household and now you're going to introduce a new baby into the family, a little common sense can go a long way in helping your pet adjust to the change.

I know that mothers worry, so first let me tell you that in all my days I have never seen a documented case of a baby being smothered by a cat. Most cats, in fact, avoid the nursery like the plague because of the high-pitched crying and other unpleasant noises.

When you first bring baby home from the hospital, do not make a fuss of introducing cat and baby. Your cat couldn't care less — until she sees all the attention baby is getting, and then she may, only may, get a little jealous. Some female cats become very protective and take on a watchdog (pardon me, watch*cat*) approach. A very few, who have been under previous stress, may react by urinating on baby's things.

Keep your cat out of the nursery for the first few months, until baby is well settled into the day's routine and your cat has grown used to all the new commotion. Don't rush things. Both baby and cat are going to be around for many years, so let your cat take things at her own pace. When you remove her from baby's area, do not shove, yell or hit or make her feel like an intruder. Just pick her up gently, give her a kiss and a hug and say, "Off you go."

When you have a few spare minutes (and that may not be often with a new baby), give your cat some quality time. This is also where the rest of your family can help out, taking care of the cat while you are very busy.

If you have brought your cat up in a gentle, loving manner, you will have no trouble. If, on the other hand, your cat has been constantly teased or taught to roughhouse and bite everything that moves, you will have to keep watch, as her natural good nature has been altered. Fortunately, though, most cats have a built-in sense that babies have to be treated differently and they tread carefully.

If your cat does react by urinating in the nursery, set up a "special room" for her (as outlined in the "Litter" section in this chapter) and keep her in there for as long as need be. Or if she is an outdoor cat, let her be outside as much as possible. She will be happier in her natural habitat until things calm down in the home.

After baby is a little older and your cat has grown used to this addition to her life, you will have no problems except the usual ones of keeping your young child from mistreating the cat. At this early age, children have no idea what they are doing; they are just curious. Again, the best place for your pet is outside or in a special room where she cannot be molested.

One important point: reread the "Litter" section earlier in this chapter and change the litter box every day. Just as with human waste, animal waste should not be left around for crawling children to get into. Where babies and little children are concerned, take no chances. (Some doctors recommend that pregnant women do not change the litter boxes. If you are pregnant, discuss this with your physician.)

CHOOSING YOUR VET

WESTERN MEDICINE has an almost mindless devotion to the surgical answer to human problems without considering its emotional impact" (Leah Cohen, *Small Expectations: Society's Betrayal of Older Women,* McClelland and Stewart, 1984). This is most certainly applicable to people medicine, but with cat medicine it is more than applicable.

When I go to a home where a depressed and psychologically abused cat lives, it cannot talk, but its owners can, and what horrific tales they have to tell.

Recently I had a client who was having problems with her cat. The first time she'd taken her kitten to the vet for its shots, the vet, fresh out of school, put the needle into the kitten's bone. The cry was horrendous. My client, not knowing any better, continued to take her cat to the same vet. Now she has a once sweet and friendly pet who hisses and spits at anyone coming through the door, thinking they've come to hurt it.

One would hope that someone who enters the field of veterinary medicine is an animal lover. But this is not always the case. Being a vet is just one more way to make a living, and today it is a very good living. If vets like animals, fine, but it doesn't seem to be a requirement for the job.

Since most people live in big cities, vets deal mostly with large dog and cat populations. Cats and dogs are vastly different in nature, and it is normal that vets should prefer one or the other. Unfortunately the cat is not the preferred pet on most vets' patient list. Cats spell trouble — they scream, they scratch, they bite. Now if half your work is with cats, it goes without saying that you should understand not only cats' illnesses but the nature of the cat. You should understand, at the very least, why the cat behaves the way she does when she visits the vet — knowledge that would help you calm her down. Alas, most vets don't understand the cat's nature and do not feel they have to. Even though hundreds of thousands of North American cats are put down each year because of behavioral problems, not one vet is formally trained to handle feline behavior. The majority of vets have no idea how to deal properly with furniture scratching, litter problems or bad diets. They recommend drugs, declawing or death.

I am not a trained vet and would never presume to offer veterinary advice. Illness is not my field of expertise — wellness is. But from my years with the Cats' Cradle, and as the Cat Psychologist, I have developed a deep understanding of the nature of cats — and of their owners. If you have a *sick* cat, the only place to go is to a vet, and fast. What I am all about is cutting down for you the traumatic, expensive and often unnecessary trips to the vet by telling you how to practice preventive cat care with common-sense, tried-and-true methods for an animal that has been around for thousands of years and whose needs have never changed.

When you look for a vet, use your good judgment, your

common sense and your love of your cat. Choose a vet with the same care you'd choose a doctor for yourself. And don't wait until your cat is ill. Before you even get your cat, visit several vets near you and get a feel for what they are about where cats are concerned. If they won't take the time to talk to you, move on. If you don't like their answers, move on. If they are reluctant to give you a tour of their premises or you don't like what you see, move on. Above all you must feel comfortable with your vet. You must feel free to discuss any problems your cat is having, or even changes in your life that seem to be affecting your cat. Far too many of my clients feel they can't talk to their vets or ask questions, and this lack of communication leads to serious problems.

Here are some questions you should ask when shopping for a vet. (Ask the vet, not the receptionist.)

- What is your opinion on declawing? (If they tell you why it is good for the cat, drop them.)

- Do you make housecalls? (If yes, you are in luck. If no, ask if they will do so in an emergency. If no again, drop them.)

- Do you like cats, and do you believe they are different from dogs? (If they don't like cats, or say they are the same as dogs, drop them.)

- Do you allow the owners to visit their hospitalized pets? (If yes, good. If no, drop them.)

- Do you yourself own a cat? (If yes, it's a good sign. If no, ask why not. There may be valid reasons, or the answer may tell you to keep shopping around.)

I know this is a lot to ask, but it is not unreasonable to expect that vets treating hundreds of cats should like them, understand them and go a little out of their way to look after them properly. They are well paid for their services, and in return you as a cat owner must get value for your money.

So now you have a vet, and his or her number kept beside your phone. When do you go? It's important to know that cats get sick quickly and go downhill quickly.

Some common trouble signs are a dull coat, refusing to eat, sleeping more and staying away from the action in the house, blood in stools or urine, diarrhea, crying out when you pick her up.

If you suspect that something is wrong, phone your vet right away, explain your cat's complete condition and then do what your vet suggests.

If your vet tells you your cat is ill, ask if she can be treated at home. Any time spent in a cage at the vet's is traumatic for your cat, and she will get better much faster in her own home, in a quiet room with the door shut. However, if you cannot cope with looking after a sick cat, with giving her pills or taking her temperature, leave her in your vet's hands. If your vet gives your cat a clean bill of health but she is still depressed and unhappy, reread my sections on play and exercise, diet and fresh air. Know that a depressed and anxious cat is wide open to physical problems, so step in before it is too late. Give your cat some quality playtime, especially if she is an indoor cat only, and get some pure, fresh food into her, and then notice the difference.

Remember Cat Rule #3, Do unto others . . . Think how you would feel if you were in your cat's shoes and what it would take to make you feel better. Then apply this to your cat.

Above all, obey Cat Rule #1: Listen to what your cat is telling you.

THE VERY YOUNG AND THE VERY OLD CAT

T HE VERY YOUNG and the very old deserve special attention, both among humans and in the cat world. I like to treat a young kitten, say eight to sixteen weeks, as if she were indeed a little human baby. When she is first brought home, someone should be there to keep her company. She will require four or five little meals a day and lots of love, and it is just not fair to bring her home, throw her in the door, give her a dish of dry food and call that kitten care.

Before you bring your kitten home, set up a cardboard carton or a small basket, put a cozy towel or sweater inside and let that be kitten's home during the day. If you can, elevate the carton so the kitten will not be subjected to drafts.

Put the kitten's bed in a quiet room (preferably your bedroom), with a clean litter box, changed every day, and a small dish of diluted milk. Keep her bed, litter box and the water and food all far from one another so the kitten does not have to eat or sleep with her nose in her bathroom.

Keep the kitten in this one room for the first few days. Then let her out to inspect, one room at a time, until she has acquainted herself with the whole area. Go slow. Your kitten will be around for a long time, so there is no need to rush anything.

Every once in a while your kitten will sit in the middle of the room and meow piteously. She misses her mother and siblings. If you pick her up and love her, she will feel so much better, and the two of you will form a close and lasting bond.

These are my recommendations for food:

AGE 8 TO 16 WEEKS

- Serve only small portions, four or five meals a day. Don't serve anything cold straight from the fridge — it can cause an upset stomach and vomiting.

- milk (half water)
- water
- baby cereal mixed with milk
- scrambled eggs, cooled, with no salt or pepper
- pureed meats (baby foods): beef, veal, chicken
- porridge
- fish, well cooked, deboned and mashed

OVER 16 WEEKS

- milk (whole)
- water
- porridge
- Cream of Wheat
- scrambled eggs
- introduce finely chopped cooked beef, chicken, liver, kidney
- junior meats (baby foods)
- cooked ground meat (for economy)
- slowly introduce vegetables such as peas and lettuce, mixed with meats
- add rice, potatoes, pasta, in very small quantities
- introduce small portions of mashed sardines, salmon, etc., mixed with small portions of vegetables

Never feed your kitten or cat dry or semimoist food.

You will soon find out what your cat does and does not like to eat. Do not force anything, but offer from time to time, and make sure she is getting the right cat proportions of mainly protein, some vegetables and very little starch.

Now for the elder statespersons of cats.

Cats act very much like people when they get old, and by old I mean fifteen or twenty years. A healthy cat will begin to show signs of aging after fifteen years; an unhealthy cat will show aging signs before fifteen, just as people usually show their age depending on how they have abused their minds and bodies.

An older cat needs peace and quiet. She should not be bothered when she's sleeping or resting, and children and teenagers should be told to leave her alone. Some older cats become very demanding in their need for affection and return to the kitten stage. If your aging cat always follows you around, meowing, and you know there is nothing physically wrong with her, pick her up and carry her around for a while. Be careful: her joints sometimes get stiff and painful.

Again I must say "you are what you eat." If your cat has lived fifteen years with a minimum of sickness, you know you are doing something right, so carry on that way. But serve smaller quantities, and offer a few more of your cat's very favorite foods around the edges. After all, your cat has been there for you all these years, through good times and bad, so now in her twilight years you will want to spoil her even more than ever.

When you go on holidays or away for the weekend, leave your cat at home. She feels safer and happier in her own surroundings. Arrange for someone to come in every day, and do not worry. An older cat sleeps even more than a younger cat, and as long as her litter is changed every day, she gets fresh food and water and someone comes in to visit for a little while, all will be well. Lugging an older cat off to the cottage in the heat every weekend or taking her on long car rides is not a good idea at this time of her life.

An older cat will appreciate being able to avoid all the noisy action of a household. When company comes, or little children, or there are noisy parties, do your pet a favor by putting her in a quiet spot and pulling the door to. This will save her having to find her own quiet spot when the noise starts.

If you treat your kitten as I have suggested, you will have a healthy, fun-loving cat. If you treat your older cat as I have suggested, you will extend her age to well over twenty and have the pleasure of her company that much longer.

THE DEATH OF YOUR CAT

INEVITABLY YOUR BELOVED companion will die, ideally peacefully of old age, but sometimes as the result of illness or misfortune. If it's a medical decision, discuss it carefully with your vet. Perhaps if your cat is suffering and there is no hope of her getting better, it would be kinder to have her put down. This is a painful decision to make, and a very personal one between you, your vet and your cat. If this is the course you choose, you should have the choice of staying with your cat as she goes to sleep. Do not feel guilty about your decision to end your cat's life. We all do what we are able, and what we think is best, and what we can handle, under the circumstances.

You can have your cat buried in a pet cemetery if you wish. Or you can know she is close by and bury her in your back yard, at least four feet down so no animal can dig her up. (Check that your local bylaws allow this.) Or you can have your cat cremated and her ashes put in your favorite vase, if that would suit you. Most vets can cremate a pet and return the ashes to you if you so desire.

The death of a cat is a traumatic experience. In fact, in the United States a few vets now use grief counselors to deal with the very real grief pet owners feel when their pets die. This is an excellent idea. Far too many grief-stricken people have been led to believe it is foolish to cry and mourn for their pet.

This is just not so. Any part of your household is a part of you, and when your pet dies a piece of you goes with her. For some the wound never heals; for others it heals in time and fond memories remain. We are all different, and we all cope with grief differently. Regardless, any sorrow has to be worked through or it can eat away at you in an unhealthy manner, never letting you move on with your life. Find a pet lover like yourself (nonanimal people simply won't under- stand) and commiserate together. If you cannot find anyone to share your grief, call me, at (416) 481-1462, and I will cry with you.

Often cat owners who have lost one cat get another to fill the gap, and they're unsatisfied. They complain that this cat is not like the one they had before. No, it isn't, I say, and it never will be.

I always tell these people to give it time and soon the new cat will work her way into their hearts and they will be in love with two cats instead of one: the one who is gone and the one who is with them. As a woman once told me when she was marrying her third husband after the first two had died, "When one door closes, another door opens." That is what life is all about, knowing that doors open and close, and how we deal with these constant changes is what counts and leads to good mental health for both ourselves and our cats.

Cats will, of course, grieve for their missing mates, especially if they are in the middle or older years and have spent much time together. This is acceptable for a certain length of time. But if it goes on too long, try to distract and stimulate your cat with new toys, catnip, lots of loving and playtime, perhaps with another cat. Your cat will probably come out of her depression in time.

If you do get another cat and the older one seems to hate her, that does not matter. Hating as well as loving can keep two cats on their toes. In time, they will come to some understanding, and probably even become fast friends.

QUESTIONS AND ANSWERS

Question

My cat is overweight. She is an indoor cat. What can I do?

Answer

First of all, take your cat off all dry or semimoist nibbling foods during the day. Feed her once in the morning and once in the evening. She should have nothing in between. If the removal of all-day nibbles does not decrease her weight, slightly reduce the amount of food she gets morning and evening.

Every day, play some of my cat games with her: increased activity will also help.

Question

If my cat fell from the sixth-floor balcony, would he land on his feet and be all right?

Answer

Although cats are a lot more agile than we are, they most certainly do not always land on their feet. If a cat falls from such a high place, depending on the angle and what he lands on he will most certainly hurt or kill himself. That is why you should be very careful with cats on balconies. If they get curious or bored, they will walk from one balcony to another, and may get lost in someone else's apartment — if they don't slip and fall on their way. They will take a swipe at a butterfly or bird going by — and over they go. So if your cat is on the balcony, sit with him and never let him out of your sight. If you are able to enclose your balcony with wire netting, so much the better.

Question

My cat is always begging for food when we are eating our meals, and my parents get mad at her and shout and hit her. They say she should not do that. I am upset by this. What do you say about it?

Answer

Your cat should be fed in the morning and in the evening, and when you are having your meals she should gently be put in another room.

When a cat smells good things to eat, it is only natural that she should want some, and no amount of yelling or hitting is going to make a bit of difference. Mealtime should be a pleasant time for your family, so just make sure your cat is not around, and all will be well. Or try putting her dinner down at the same time you start to eat yours. If she has a tasty meal of her own, she won't be interested in what you're eating.

Question

Why am I always hearing about cats getting inside car motors and being killed, and what can I do to prevent this?

Answer

Cats will do this in the winter to get warm, or they may go there to hide from a dog or someone who is frightening them. If you are worried about this, lift the hood of your car before you start the engine. This way, you will never have to live with a dead cat on your conscience.

Question

My cat is an indoor cat, but once in a while I would like to take him out for fresh air and grass. How can I do this?

Answer

I think it is a very good idea, with one big *if* — if your cat likes it. Forget the idea if after one or two tries your cat is absolutely terrified and gets no pleasure out of it.

Let your cat be free — never use a leash or a harness, which makes your cat feel restrained and stops him from enjoying being outdoors. Start out in the back yard or in a quiet spot. If your cat is more curious than afraid, do not overdo it, and repeat on a daily basis. Always supervise him. If a dog or something else that frightens him approaches, pick up your cat and protect him. One good scare and the walking will be over for good.

If you know you want to do this regularly and have just got a kitten, get him used to you and your indoor surroundings first, say about six months — and then try him outside. The younger he is the more adaptable he is to a new lifestyle.

Question

We have had our cat since my son was two. I thought he would grow out of teasing the cat in a mean way. He hasn't. He is now eight, and the mean treatment can sometimes be very cruel. What shall I do?

Answer

Any child who shows such traits should have some professional help immediately. This mean streak must be dealt with for the child's and the cat's sake. Although younger children don't always realize they may be hurting a pet, don't let cruel treatment to cats continue. Always discuss it with your doctor.

Question

What do I have to be careful of around the house that could be poisonous to my cat?

Answer

Do not use a spray of any kind near your cat. This includes hair spray, perfumes and deodorants as well as room fresheners and insecticides. None of these strong chemicals is good for your cat to inhale or get in her eyes. If you must use any of these sprays, make sure your cat's food and water are not nearby.

If your cat likes to drink water out of the bathtub or the kitchen or bathroom sinks, do not use strong chemicals to clean them and always rinse thoroughly.

If you must spray the house for fleas, do it one room at a time. Your cat must not be allowed to breathe in the deadly chemicals.

Question

My cat is constantly licking his genital area. What does this mean?

Answer

You should take him to the vet immediately. He could have a bladder infection and should be treated at once before it gets any worse.

Question

What do you think about flea collars for cats?

Answer

I do not like flea collars of any kind. We should try to eliminate all chemicals in the cat's life. Some cats are allergic to the chemicals. As well, while the cat is eating and drinking, the chemicals are oozing out into her food and water.

Question

My cat has been on one brand of cat food for a long time and now refuses to eat it or anything else for that matter. What should I do to tempt him to eat?

Answer

Cats love variety in their food and will soon be bored and depressed if you keep them on one food for too long. Try tempting him with cooked liver, cooked fish (well mashed) or any of the baby-food meats. Warmed milk and cooked eggs will also get his tastebuds going again in a nonchemical way.

Question

What is the main difference between male and female cats when they are spayed and neutered?

Answer

The female is no longer able to have kittens and the male is no longer able to make kittens. Spaying and neutering also cut down on the tendency of both males and females to wander. Thus they become quite happy in their own back yards, though the male remains territorial and sometimes aggressive with other male cats. I find that neutered males are usually a little more laid-back with people, and spayed females, with people, are just a little more careful.

Question

I live in an apartment, and although my cat and I are very happy together, I wonder if I should get another one to keep him company?

Answer

This is a question I am often asked, as people think their cats must be lonely at home all day alone. But this is not the case. A cat will usually sleep all day, and as long as you are home most nights and weekends he gets just enough attention. If you are away all the time, you will be making two cats unhappy instead of one.

Question

I have three cats and they will not stop scratching my furniture. What can I do? They do not go outside.

Answer

The main thing is to give them fun and interesting alternatives so they'll forget about your furniture. You can buy or make a cat tree. This is a stand that goes from floor to ceiling with many perches on the way up. It is very solid and is usually covered in broadloom. Your cats can run up and down, sit and sun, scratch, and chase each other. They love it.

Also, you could build a foot-wide shelf at ceiling level around one sunny room with steps or a ramp up to it in one corner. Your cats can then zing around the room high up.

FIVE

New Frontiers:
You Can Make a Difference

··

I T SEEMS ONLY RIGHT that we strive to help the cat, for the cat aids us in ways we're not always aware of. Do you know someone who is ill in hospital? Do you have a friend trying to recover from alcohol or drug addiction? These people can be vastly helped with a little daily cat therapy.

Studies have shown that the presence of cats can lower blood pressure, reduce anxiety, uplift spirits and generally take the ill person's mind off his troubles and himself. Consequently, in developed countries worldwide, cats are now being taken into sterile hospital rooms and the inhuman environments of many institutions, with exciting results. The elderly who have been left to die in chronic-care facilities and retirement homes and have lost interest in everything perk up at the sight of a cat. The sick and hospital-bound, adults and children alike, light up at the sight of the friendly, gentle cat. Mentally ill people may not trust their fellow humans (sometimes for good reason), but they will open up to a cat.

From autistic children to prison inmates, with whom often nothing can be done, the cat is up to his old tricks — making people feel good.

In Windsor, Ontario, nurse Sharon McMahon started up a group called the Companion Animal Visitation Program. She and her forty volunteers take a variety of pets to visit the residents of thirty-two institutions in the Windsor area. She says, "The therapeutic effect a friendly animal has on people is sometimes astonishing."

And research shows you don't have to be sick to benefit. In fact, owning a cat can *reduce* the risk of illness. Dr. Alan Secord, a well-known Canadian veterinarian for fifty-eight years, has often talked about the bond between people and their pets. During his many years of practice, he says, he has seen over and over the psychological importance of animals to their owners and how the owners are helped by having their animals close by. Some studies have shown that people with pets have fewer blood pressure and heart problems and generally live longer, healthier lives. It seems to help having a pet you can talk to, care for, touch and who can give you unqualified affection.

So if your cat is a good traveler, pop him into his carrying case and take him on a visit, knowing that "a little bit of cat magic makes the medicine go down." You will be surprised — and warmed — by the results.

(Two cautions: If your cat does not travel well, don't do this. A frightened cat cannot work that needed magic. And make sure the institution you're visiting permits pets.)

The wonderful story of Koko the gorilla at the San Francisco Zoo illustrates the cat helping us in another way. This gorilla fell in love with All Ball, a little kitten. Observing the maternal instinct this kitten brought out in Koko enabled Dr. Francine Patterson and her team to further their ongoing studies of gorilla behavior. The cat does it again, always contributing and helping, no matter what country, what situation, in hundreds of extraordinary ways.

Many countries in the modern world are fast becoming made up of two classes: the very rich and the very poor. The middle class is gradually slipping away. The result is terrible economic problems for many families.

The cost of having a cat spayed or neutered by a vet is often prohibitively high for people who have to watch over their pennies. The cost of having a cat fixed at an animal shelter or the Humane Society, although probably half as much, is still too high for poor people and those heading in that direction. When it comes down to a choice between food and rent or having your cat fixed there is no question which comes first. And when the kittens come and the whole situation is out of hand, they are all given up for adoption, or all too often killed.

My proposal is to set up free spay and neuter clinics. This is the only way people with little funds will have access to this necessary operation. Just as doctors and lawyers donate their services to people who cannot afford them, vets worldwide should set time aside when people know they can come and get their cats done. Such a service can be provided for people with old age pensions, on welfare or unemployment insurance, single parents — the list goes on. You can see that if free clinics were set up, hundreds of thousands of cats' lives would be saved, and the same number of cats would be spared from being born into a life of misery.

Whether people should have pets when they can't afford them is not the point. When parents see their sons or daughters in love with an animal, what can they do? It is very painful for them to deprive their children of such an important part of growing up just because there isn't the money for spaying and neutering. Vets who are well established and caring could hardly refuse some of their time for such a worthwhile cause.

I like everything we do for the cat to be natural and simple, and I do not want us to change the cat in any way we do not have to. But letting cats have litter after litter of kittens with no one to care for them is morally inexcusable in this day and age. And it is again morally inexcusable that professionals do not donate their services to an animal who enables them to make an excellent living.

Speak to your vet about it — now.

Just as shelters for battered women are being set up, I would like to see "safe houses" for cats set up for those cats who are stressed out, abandoned or just plain old. Instead of killing them, we could put them into a caring home atmosphere, with a cat lover in charge. Such shelters could be run much the way I ran my Cats' Cradle. I had a small bungalow, with a screened-in back porch where my guest cats could get fresh air and exercise, and the cats had the run of the house. They were free, natural and happy.

These shelters would be perfect places to train feline behaviorists. And the homes could be sponsored by the people who have benefited so well from the cat all these years — corporate pet food and litter manufacturers.

The Jaguar car company now sponsors a program to save African jaguars from extinction. Since they have profited from using the jaguar as a symbol all these years, they feel it is the least they can do. Pet food and litter manufacturers would score a lot of points if they did indeed save cats' lives by helping set up safe houses. The houses would not have to be expensive or elaborate, since cats need only clean space and loving attendants. And I would be only too glad to offer my services as a consultant in establishing such an operation.

If you agree that this would be a good idea, write to your cat-food or litter manufacturer and tell them so. We owe that great money-maker, that great comforter, the cat, better treatment. Get that letter off today.

The "greening" of our products to make them environmentally friendly has now begun — at long last. We are now rethinking our whole consumer society. We are thinking of ways to recycle so that we can save our planet. The kitchen is the first place to start. We are fast learning to reuse containers and coffee filters, to switch to homemade cleansers and cloth diapers. And just as we are organizing our kitchen for our family, so must we now include our family pet.

It is morally unacceptable to manufacture or to buy food

that is strictly for cats *if* what you have in your own kitchen is fresh, nutritious, fulfills your cat's needs and, in many instances, would otherwise be thrown out. "Designer cat food" is wrong in a world of mass hunger, disappearing rain forests and pollution.

You must take the feeding of your cat into your own hands, and this starts with the "greening" of your kitchen. My "Food" section in chapter 4 tells you what combination of foods you can feed your cat. Use what you're eating that day, or use leftovers, and turn it into cat food that is fresh and healthy. This new (in fact it's old) approach to feeding your cat will save on energy, cut down on the waste of unnecessary packaging and be a small but important contribution on your part to cleaning up our environment. Plus you'll have a happier, healthier cat with fewer behavioral problems and fewer trips to the vet for you.

These practical ideas would save the lives of thousands of cats and eventually lead to our getting hold of an out-of-control cat crisis. Such new cat concepts are also controversial, and that is good. Controversy, new ideas, seeing things in a different way, trying out new approaches — without any of this, we have no progress.

If we in the nineties want to go down in the annals of "cat history" as having been caring, compassionate and concerned about animal rights, we must start right now to get our "cat act" together. Hundreds of millions of cat owners worldwide can make a difference.

If your cat has a behavioral problem, you can write to me, from anywhere in the world, and I will do my best to help you and your cat.

> The Cat Psychologist
> P.O. Box 4, Station Z
> Toronto, Ontario
> Canada M5N 2Z3

FURTHER READING

Bush, Dr. Barry. *The Cat Care Question and Answer Book*.
London: Orbis Publishing, 1981; New York: Simon
and Schuster, 1983.

Fournier, Katou, and Jacques Lehmann. *All Our Cats*.
New York: E. P. Dutton, 1985.

Lawson, Pate and Tony Lawson. *The Cat-Lover's Cookbook*.
Pownal, VT: Storey Communications, 1986.

Loxton, Howard. *Guide to the Cats of the World*.
London: Treasure Press, 1983.

Riddle, Roz. *The City Cat: How to Live Healthy and Happily
with Your Indoor Pet*. New York: Fawcett, 1987.

Thies, Dagmar. *Cat Care*. Neptune City, NJ:
TFH Publications, 1980.

INDEX

Page numbers in **bold type** indicate question and answer sections.

Absence,
  long term, 41, 45–46, **70**, 74, 75–76, 118
  short term, 21, 23, 41, 45, **70**, 75–76, 118
  See also Pet-sitter; Traveling
Aging, 117–18
Aluminum foil, as deterrent, 99, 101
Anger, signs of, 22
Animal shelter, 81, 84, 109
Anxiety, signs of, 22, **31**, **66**, 104
  See also Scratching, people; Stress
Apartments, **68**, 97, **126**
  balconies, **121**
  and "no pets" clause, 75
  See also Indoor cats; Stresses; Territory

Baby, 77–78, 110–12
  See also Children
Baby foods, 93, 94, 95, 117, **125**
Begging for food, **122**
Behavior, 18–22, **28**, 83
  natural, 28
  natural, frustration of, 35, 37, 65–66
  need to understand, 10, 23, 24, 35, 37–38, 79, 95–96, 104, 113
  and neutering/spaying, 76, 105, **125–26**
Behavioral problems, 23, 24–25, 37, 38, 49, **66–70**, 78, 91
  chewing, 59–60, 61–62
  chewing houseplants, **66–68**
  declawing and, 26, 39, 63, 64, 106, 107
  diet and, 25, 90–91, 98

fighting, 60–61, 65
litter problem, 37, 39, 57–59, 63, 95, 96–101
returning to former home, 62
spraying, 54, 64–65, 111–12
See also Stresses
Biting, **31**, 63–64, 111
Boarding, 45, **66–67**
Bones, in food, 93, 117
Breeds, 83–84
Butter, 93, 95
  buttering paws, 51

Carriers, 84–85
  fear of entering, **69**
Cat, acquiring, 80–82
  fitting into human lifestyle, 24, 83, 110
  and freedom, 17, 21, 35, 47, 76, 110
  modern role of, 17, 24, 37
  nature of, 19, 27, 28, 38, 45, 47, 51, 54, 81, 95–96
  needs of, 17, 19, 23, 25–26, 45, 48, 65, 76–77
  and therapy, 131–32
Cat breeders, 82, 84
Cat doors, **29**
Cat grass, **67**, 93
Cat-person relationship, 17, 19, 23, 27, 28, 50, **67**, **69–70**, 73, 74, 75, 81, 132
  cat's dependence, 73, 75, 99
  owner's dependence, 17, 18, 24, 44, 176
  compromise in, 24, 28, 38, 40, 79–80, 102
  establishing, 52, 84, 116
  qualities of ideal owner, 76, 79
Cats, interrelationships, **30**, 53, 65, 120
Cheese, 93, 95
Chemicals, 92, 97, **124**, **125**

in food, 90
Chicken, 93, 95, 117
Children, 78, 83–84, 108–10, 112
    and noise, 77
    and play, 78, 103
    and teasing, 103, **123–24**
    value of cat for, 24, 109, 110
    See also Baby; Stresses
Crying, 20, 83
    kittens, 116
    older cat, 118

Dangers, balconies, **121**
    cars, **122**
    poisons, 92, **124**
    toys, 103–4
Death, 119–20
    See also Grieving
Declawing, 24, 26, 41, 42, 78, 89,
    105–8
    See also Behavioral problems;
    Stresses
Depression, 23, 40, 49, 91, 115
Diet, and behavioral problems, 91
    and health, 25, 40, 55, 90–91,
    92, 93, 94, **121**
    recommended, 93
    recommended for kittens, 116–
    17
    See also Food

Eggs, 93, 95, 117, **125**
Exercise, 19, 43–44, 75, 78, 83,
    89, 101–4, **126–27**
    and health, 102, **121**
    See also Play
Eye contact, 20

Falling, **121**
Fear of people, 27, 28, **66**, 79, 109,
    112
Feeding, 22, **29**
    frequency, 93, 116, **121**
    older cat, 118
Fish, 93, 95, 117, **125**
Flea collars, **125**

Flea spray, **124**
Food, 89–95, 134–35
    additives, 90
    commercial, 24, 40, 55, 90, 91–
    92, 94, 135
    dry and semimoist, 57, **70**, 90,
    94, 98, 117, **121**
    freshness of, 20, 25, **29**, 89, 90,
    95
    scratching near, 20, **29**
    variety of, 25, 42, 90, 94, **125**
    See also Aging; Diet; Kittens

Games, 102–3
    See also Exercise; Play, Toys
Grieving, among cats, **30**, 120
    for your cat, 119–20
Grooming, 75, 84

Habitat, need to replace what is lost
    from, 18, 23, 35, 37, 40, 44,
    65–66, 107
Health, signs of, 82–83
    See also Diet; Stress; Veterinar-
    ian
Humane Society. *See* Animal shel-
    ter

Illness, 23, 49, 75, 115, 119
    common signs of, 115
    and eating, 94
    See also Urinary tract disorders;
    Veterinarian
Indoor cats, 18, 23, 24, 40, 41, 84
    and diet, 40, 90–91
    and exercise, 43–44, 75, 83,
    102
    going outside, **123**
Introducing new people, 52
Introducing other cats, 52–53

Kittens, acquiring, 80–82
    behavior, 26–27, **28**, 83
    and biting, **31**, 63
    bringing home, 84–85, 116
    feeding, 93, 116–17

Kitty Calls, 9–10
Kitty mills, 81–82
Kneading, 22

Leashes, 41, 47, **123**
Leashing bylaws, 17–18, 46–47
Lettuce, **67**, 93, 117
Licking of genital area, **124**
Litter box, behavioral problems
    and, 25–26, 95–96
    and children, 112
    cleaning, 51, 78, 89, 97
    hooded, 96
    number of, 78, 96, 97
    placement of, 78, 96–97, 116
    plastic liners, 97
    and privacy, 64–65, 78,
    95–96
Litter problem. *See* Behavioral
    problems
Liver, 93, 94–95, 117, **125**

Meat, 92, 93, 95, 117
    cooking, 92, 93, 94–95
Milk, 92, 93, 94, 95, 116, 117,
    125
Moving, 50–53, 62

Neutering, 48, 78, 81, 89, 104–5
    and behavior, 76, 105, **125–26**
    free clinics, 132–33
    kittens, 85

Obesity, 57, 93, 102, **121**
Outdoor cats, 17–18, 59, 85, 101–
    2
    in new home, 51
    See also Leashing bylaws
Overvetting, 24, 26, 41, 42–43

Pasta, 93, 117
Pet shops, 82
Pet-sitter, 45-46, **69**, **70**, 74, 76,
    118
    See also Absence
Petting, 21, 22, 75, 109, 132

Picking up a cat, 52, 103, 118
    method, 110
Play, 42, 43, 65, **66**, **67**, 75, 101–
    104, 108, **121**
    biting during, **31**
    See also Exercise
Poisons, 92, 97, **124**
Potatoes, 93, 117
Preventative care, 43, 89, 98, 115
Protein, 93, 94, 95, 117
    See also Meat
Punishment, ineffectiveness of,
    26–28, 79, **122**
    See also Teaching
Purring, 22

Rice, 117
Roughhousing, **68**, 78, 103, 104,
    109
    danger of, **31**, 111

"Safe houses" for cats, 133–34
Salmon, 93, 95, 117
Sardines, 93, 95, 117
Scratching, 26, 28, 102, 108, **126–
    27**
    people, 52, 63, 110
Scratching post, 28, 78, 102, 107,
    108, **126**
Seafood, 93, 95, 117
Snacks, 57, 93, 94, **121**
Spaying, 48, 78, 81, 89,
    104–5
    and behavior, 76, 105, **125–26**
    free clinics, 132–33
    kittens, 85
Smell, sense of, 20, 26, 53, 56, 90,
    96
    and litter problem, 100–101
    and scratching, 108
    See also Stresses
"Special room" routine, 50–51,
    52–53, 63, 77
    for behavioral problems, 59–
    60, 64, 65
    for kittens, 85, 116

for litter problem, 98–101,
  111–12
when moving, 50–53, 62
Starch, 93, 117
Stress, and cat "safe houses," 133–
  34
  and illness, 23, 40, 43, 49, 55,
    56, 74, 91, 115
  signs of, 37, 81
  See also Behavioral problems
Stresses, 24, 41
  being restrained, 41, **66**
  boarding, 45, **66–67**
  boredom, 41, 49, 63, 65, **67**,
    75
  change of environment, 45, 48–
    53, 59–60, 62, 76–77
  children, 38, 77, 78, 83–84,
    103, 109–10, 111, 112, **123–
    24**
  declawing, 39, 41, 63, 64, 107
  deprivation of natural habitat,
    17, 23, 24, 35, 37, 41, 65
  dirty litter box, 25–26, 41, 58,
    98
  of indoor cat, 40–41, 65, **67**,
    75, 77
  lack of space, 61–62, 65, **68**, 75,
    79
  loneliness, 39, 41, 44, 45, 49,
    63, 65
  natural, 65
  noise, 38–39, 46, 54, 55, 58,
    64–65, 77, 118
  other cats, 52–53, 60–61, 64–
    65, 77, 79
  poor diet, 39, 40, 41, 55, 57,
    63, 64, **67**, **125**
  punishment, 27–28, 63–64, **67**
  smells, 55–56, 61, 77
  spaying/neutering, 48
  strangers, 46, 52, 77
  surgery, 41
  teasing, 39, 63, **68**
  territorial, 52, 60–61, 64–65
  tobacco smoke, 55–56, **68**, 77

traveling, 59–60, **68–69**, 76
  at vet's, 41, 115
  See also Moving; Overvetting
Sucking, **30**

Tail, 22, 104
Talking to cats, 20–21, **31**, 75, 132
Teaching, by example, 27, **30**, 79
  See also Punishment
Territory, amount required, 62,
  68, 75, 126
  establishing, 51, 52–53, 57–58
  need for, 36, 61–62, 65
  trespassing, 52, 60–61
  See also Stresses
Toys, 42, 75, 103–4
Tranquilizers, 43, 64, 65, **68**
Traveling, **68–69**, 76
  with older cat, 118
Tuna, 93

Urinary tract disorders, 58, 64, 94,
  98, **124**

Vegetables, 93, 117
Veterinarian, 112–15
  choosing, 113–15
  and euthanasia, 119
  when to go, 113, 115
  See also Overvetting

Water, 78, 92, 117, **124**